Exploring the
Oregon Coast
by Car

A Guide to Special Places & Activities

Marje Blood

The Writing Works,
Division of Morse Press, Inc.
Seattle, WA

Gordon Soules Book Publishers
Vancouver, B.C., Canada

Library of Congress Cataloging in Publication Data

Blood, Marje,
   Exploring the Oregon coast by car.

   Includes index.
   1. Oregon—Description and travel—1951—Guide-books.
2. Automobiles—Road guides—Oregon.
I. Title.
F874.3.B56 1980   917.95'0443   80-25484
ISBN 0-916076-41-5 (U.S.)

Second Printing
Copyright © 1980 by Marje Blood
All Rights Reserved
Manufactured in the United States
Published by   The Writing Works, Inc.
                 Division of Morse Press, Inc.
                 417 East Pine St.
                 Seattle, WA 98122

ISBN: 0-916076-41-5 (U.S.)
Library of Congress Number: 80-25484
Published in Canada by Gordon Soules Book Publishers
   325-355 Burrard Street
   Vancouver, B.C., Canada V6C 2G8
ISBN : 0-919574-38-6 (Canada)

Contents

ACKNOWLEDGMENTS

My grateful thanks goes to these people who helped me see this book through to completion: Sylvia and Jerry Towne, Val Thoenig, Kim Hill, Jim and June White, Ione Reed, Mary Lou Skinner, Renny Strahota; and especially to Mimi Bell.

Photo Credits

Cover, Anne Hinds; Mimi Bell, 51, 78; Marje Jorgensen, 110, 132 (bottom); Mary Jean Kelso, 176; Oregon State Hwy. Dept., 36, 54, 59; Ione Reed, 7, 23, 31, 157; James Seeley White, 2, 27, 33, 47, 53; Doug Wilson, 150; Kathy Moritz, 165; all others, Marje Blood.

Foreword

Appropriately Marje Blood begins her book with a review of that famed expedition across the continent to the Oregon coast by Lewis and Clark's "Corps of Discovery" nearly 200 years ago. Her own exploration by car is a small tour of discovery in itself. From the mouth of the Columbia River to the California border, she has discovered the *specials*, the exciting surprises, the off-beat nooks and crannies that a woman with imagination and unending curiosity does find.

She takes us to meet the artists and craftsmen who work to the rhythms of the sea in glass and wood and clay and gems gathered from the sand. She discovers the nostalgic and the new, she tells us about those first dauntless adventurers who came by sailing ship, and about how modern machines whisk cranberries out of seashore bogs. She finds magic in a toy factory and excitement in swooshing up and down the sand dunes of Oregon's own Sahara, and she directs us to the best clam chowder, the most special scampi, and the freshest coffee on the route. Much more than a guide, her book is a celebration of the lovely Oregon Coast.

MIMI BELL

Exploring the Oregon Coast by Car

This is a book about some special places on the Oregon Coast. It's not about the "best" places, nor the "most popular" ones, nor about the "most unusual." And not all of the special places are included. (Every place on the coast of Oregon is special in its own way.) The ones I've written about are those that, for one reason or another, seemed to belong in the book I wanted to write.

"Exploring the Oregon Coast by Car" isn't a traditional guidebook, although it can be used as such. It has more writing than most guides—stories about interesting people and places and events that too often get lost in the listings.

It takes courage to even think about writing an Oregon Coast guidebook, given the numbers of excellent ones in the bookshops. Three years ago, when the possibilty came up, the prospect seemed doubly formidable. The shadows of increasing inflation and the energy crisis were clouding the horizon like the great black storms that roll in from the Pacific Ocean during the winter.

It seemed likely that for most families the popular weekend fly-by down the coast would give way to longer vacations in one area, where they would have time to seek out and

Misty Neahkahnie Mountain, viewed across Nehalem Bay, was considered by the Indians to be a dwelling place of coyote god Talapus.

browse small shops and galleries and parks which aren't always mentioned in books. With a week or two of lazy living in prospect, they might even have time to read.

I decided to write a "nooks and crannies" guidebook; one that would accommodate the changing patterns that were sure to develop in vacation and recreation travel as a result of fuel shortages and escalating prices. The book is composed of eight sections, each focusing on a specific area. Within each division, the attractions which make that region unique are featured. These sections are separated by general stories which pertain to the coast as a whole. In effect, the book is a series of regional magazines bound together to make a book which covers the 350-mile Oregon coastline.

I began by concentrating on small places, visiting with shop owners, artists, and craftspeople who work and live along Oregon's Pacific boundary, so the book is also about some very special people. But it soon became obvious that I could not write this book without including those places which have become landmarks over the years. I could never explain an Oregon Coast without stories about the Sea Lion Caves, or Bruce's Candy Kitchen. I tried to see these veteran attractions from a new perspective in spite of a shortage of new information. As the bits and pieces of familiar detail interwove with new facts, a total picture of Oregon's magnificent coast began to emerge reflecting a region of natural beauty and fulfilling life styles unique to this country, and perhaps in the world.

Many special places are not included in the book. Space limitations imposed difficult choices. I know the others are there. If your special place has not been profiled in these pages, I'm sorry. I hope you enjoy mine.

Beverly Beach seven miles north of Newport has an awesome collection of driftwood. The state park, one of several which offer year-around camping, has 150 sites, more than 100 trailer sites, plus picnic facilities. Additional recreational accommodations include a utility building and a theater.

The Corps of Discovery

The expedition commissioned by President Thomas Jefferson under the leadership of Army Captain Meriwether Lewis and William Clark was one of the most ambitious voyages of exploration in the history of the United States. Jefferson's general commission to map the virgin wilderness routes also included explicit instructions to follow the rivers flowing west above the Missouri River system in search of the fabled Northwest Passage. The diaries kept by the two men comply in minute detail with his further instructions to record their observations of natural history, botanical and zoological information, and the appearance and customs of the native peoples they encountered along the way.

The 45 men departed St. Louis without fanfare on May 14, 1804, and for five months worked their way upstream 1,600 miles to the Mandan villages in the Dakota territory, where they wintered in Fort Mandan, constructed by the party near the Indian villages. This neighborliness during the long winter months caused the leaders some concern over their men fraternizing with the attractive Mandan women.

In April of 1805, having engaged the services of Toussaint Charboneau and his young Shoshone wife Sacajawea as interpreters and guides, the party—now down to 29 members—spent the summer crossing the continental divide and on August 11 made contact with the Shoshones. Caching their canoes by filling them with rocks and sinking them in the river, they bought horses from relatives of Sacajawea and pushed ahead, anxious to finish the mountain crossings before the winter snows.

Near the end of September Nez Perce on the Clearwater River affirmed that the Columbia River would take them to the Pacific. Building canoes of cedar and leaving their horses with the Indians, the party began the final leg of the journey. On November 7 Clark recorded they had sighted the ocean, and on December 3 carved his name and the date into a pine tree overlooking the Pacific on the north side of the Columbia.

For 10 days, battered by winds and tides which set their camp in a small cove afloat, the leaders observed the natives crossing the stormy bay in their canoes in spite of mountainous tides. Believing the south side of the river offered a better site for a winter stay, the company took advantage of a brief clearing spell to make the crossing themselves.

Three miles up the river now named for them, Lewis and Clark began to build their winter quarters of logs and shingles in pouring rain which seldom let up, and then for only a few hours at a time. By Christmas they were under cover and trading with nearby Indians. Fort Clatsop was named after the most attractive of the nearby tribes, the Clatsops, who were a source of help during the remainder of the stay.

They spent the winter drying elk meat, making clothes to replace their rotting buckskins, tanning skins of smaller animals for blankets, and refining salt upon the cairn set up at the beach 15 miles to the south. Statistics rebuild the skeleton of their story: during the time they spent at Fort Clatsop they killed 131 elk, 20 deer, otter and beaver. There were only 12 out of the 106 days spent there that they were not drenched with steady downpours of coastal rain. But, except for petty thievery, they had no trouble with their Indian neighbors.

Finally, on March 23, 1806, they began the reverse journey, arriving back in St. Louis on Tuesday, September 23, having lost only one man on the demanding journey of 28 months, who died of an incurable illness.

Today at a national memorial maintained by the United States Department of the Interior, Fort Clatsop has been reconstructed on the exact site where, a hundred years earlier, the rotting logs of the original fort were already

The replica of Fort Clatsop, whose buildings housed the 32 members of the Lewis and Clark expedition through the winter of 1805-1806, is located 4½ miles southwest of Astoria on the site of the original. The 125 acres that comprise the Fort Clatsop National Memorial also include the spring which provided the group's water supply and the landing where the boats were sheltered during the storms which assailed them through the winter. The 50-foot square stockade is centered by a small parade ground bordered by two rows of log cabins that served as living quarters and storage units. The restored site and buildings were rebuilt following the detailed drawings and instructions contained in the daily journals kept by the leaders of the "Corps of Discovery" during their voyage of exploration, one of the most important in the history of the United States.

overgrown with vines. The site's location was preserved in the memory of local residents, however, and exact replicas of the buildings were completed in 1955 as part of the Lewis and Clark Centennial Celebration.

The replica, following explicit plans drawn in the diaries, is a 50-foot square centered by a strip of parade ground which is paralleled by two rows of small log cabins with shed roofs of shingles slanting toward the center of the enclosure.

The fort's safety assured by guards having a clear view of the entire roof, the enclosure was completed by rows of logs, sharpened to points, which formed the stockade and entry gates. The men slept eight to a cabin in bunks; the Charboneaus were allotted one room, the two leaders shared a cabin, and the officers' quarters were adjacent to the storage units where their precious supplies were kept under lock and key. Each room had a rude fireplace, and they were built to ensure protection from the incessant rain.

The grounds are kept in their natural state, preserving the paths to the spring and to the canoe landing and the slough where the party's five canoes were berthed when not in use.

Supplementing the visual presentation of the actual quarters which housed the company through the winter of 1805-1806 are the exhibits and books and maps at the visitors' center, plus a half-hour film narration by TV star Lorne Green. During the summer park rangers dressed in authentic costumes enact day-to-day activities of the original party while demonstrating the frontier arts which were necessary to their survival—candle making, tanning, beadwork, making moccasins, splitting shakes, curing jerky—as part of an annual program.

Within a 25-mile radius are other historical reminders of the Lewis and Clark stay: in addition to the Salt Cairn at Seaside are Ecola State Park site near Cannon Beach where Captain Clark took Sacajawea to show her the beached whale, and the trail over Tillamook Head which leads to them. Across the river on the Washington side of the Columbia at

Fort Canby State Park is another visitors' center which presents the Lewis and Clark story.

Picnic tables are provided near the Fort Clatsop center, and overnight camping is available at Fort Stevens State Park a few miles away, providing fine camping facilities of 600 spaces, restrooms, electric stoves, fireplaces, and picnic tables all year around.

Winter or summer, a visit to Fort Clatsop Memorial offers an extraordinary opportunity to see the conditions under which the expedition survived.

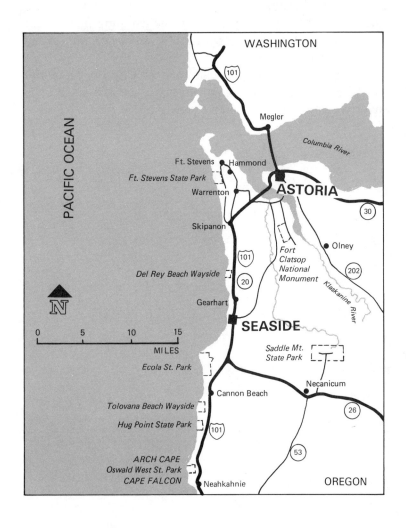

Astoria
Warrenton
Seaside
Cannon Beach

ASTORIA

Astoria is, without qualification, the historic center of Oregon. Since 1792, when Captain Robert Gray found courage to maneuver his ship, the *Columbia*, across the formidable bar and into the river that bears its name, the area has been a focal point for "firsts" in the country's history.

Following the sojourn of the Lewis and Clark "Corps of Discovery" the winter of 1805-1806, John Jacob Astor, the New York financier, organized the Pacific Fur Company in 1810 to establish an American Fur trade on the Columbia River. One half of the dual expedition brought Astor's trade ship the *Tonquin* around Cape Horn loaded with the supplies while an overland party crossed in the tracks of Lewis and Clark. The *Tonquin* party arrived six months before the land party and built Fort Astoria in 1811—the first permanent American settlement in the West.

It was a daring commercial venture but the timing was poor; the War of 1812 made the arrival of relief ships for the colony chancy. The Fort was subsequently taken by the British and renamed Fort George. The Americans regained' control in 1846 in the horsetrading that accompanied the end of the joint occupation of the Northwest by England and the United States when the boundary between the two countries was established at the 49th parallel. The Fort is now partially restored on its original site at 15th and Exchange Streets in Astoria and is open to the public.

The first post office west of the Rocky Mountains was started in 1847 by John Shively on a site near the restored Fort Astoria. A year later the first customs house on the Pacific Coast was begun when John Adair recorded the arrival of the first vessel to officially enter the Port of Astoria on April 3, 1849.

The Astoria Column

Symbol for the historical events which have centered around the city is the Astoria Column towering 125 feet atop Coxcomb Hill. Built by the Great Northern Railroad to complete a series of six historic monuments along its right of way, it was originally planned as a giant flagstaff holding an outsize American flag. However, the architect of the monument suggested a tower to be designed by Italian artist Attilio Pusterla.

The impressive tower topped by an observation balcony is finished with a series of spiral panels which depict the historic events which occurred in the region. The artist chose to finish the exterior in graffito, a form of bas-relief produced by layering white stucco over a darker concrete base and literally scratching the designs through the top layer.

It was finished in 1926 at a cost of $27,000, which was shared by the railway and a contribution from Vincent Astor, the great-grandson of the city's founder. Repaired and refinished 10 years later, the tower still requires periodic maintenance to keep deterioration to a minimum. In 1975 interior supports were constructed to slow down the cracking which has gradually worsened over the years.

The view from the top offers a spectacular vista of the Pacific beyond the mouth of the Columbia, fed by a network of rivers; several towns which have grown up along the Columbia; and, when the weather is clear, Mt. Hood and the temperamental Mt. St. Helens.

Even standing at the foot of the unique structure the view of the city and its waterfront 735 feet below is impressive. For the past few years the tower has been lighted at night, making it visible several miles out to sea.

More than 75,000 visitors a year make the trip up Coxcomb Drive to the park which surrounds the colorful monument. And nearby is another item for the city's record of "firsts"—the antenna system which carried the nation's first cable TV transmission in 1948.

The Big Fire of 1922

On December 8, 1922, the city was subjected to a traumatic series of "firsts" when, at 1:45 a.m., fire swept beneath the pilings of the waterfront business district centered along 10th Street. The business blocks, built on pilings over the river, were made with plank "basements" beneath the floors where coal for heating the establishments was stored. By the end of the second day the entire downtown business area was a mass of glowing coal fires, including a number of "red light" houses. Patients from St. Mary's Hospital were evacuated to the high school, safely out of the fire's path. The coal burned for days, business records were destroyed, and more than one merchant sent bills for amounts thought to be due, accepting customers' corrected statements as basis for payment.

Safes from many businesses fell through the burning floors into the smoldering coal piles. It was 10 days before local shopowners could inspect their papers to see what had survived when they were finally opened by "professional" safebreakers.

The black snags of pilings which prickle the river's edge along the waterfront are reminders of the total destruction of the town's historic commercial area over half a century ago.

Astoria Hotel

The pink shell of the historic Astoria Hotel stands like an aging dowager on the hillside overlooking the modernistic

Maritime Museum building on the waterfront.

The elegant old building was abandoned in 1968, and the windows removed. Tentative restoration plans call for shops on the street levels, and living units on the upper floors. In the meantime, it is protected from destruction by being placed on the National Registry of Historic Places.

The Waterfront

Astoria's waterfront is the city's heartbeat. In keeping with its founding as a trade center, its development has taken place along the river which is its lifeline to sources of commerce. But fluctuating conditions in the world and advancing technology have brought changes to the dock area as old businesses have been crowded out by new ones.

Interspersed among established companies which have weathered the ups and downs of the city's fortunes are newcomers in remodeled warehouses offering services and merchandise that would have been unheard of as dock-based enterprises a few years ago.

Pier 11

Most notable perhaps is the Pier 11 complex developed in renovated buildings between 10th and 11th Streets by Darrell Davis and his family. **The Black Murex** is a wonderland of nautical gifts and accessories for those who love the sea and its treasures. Shells of course: baskets full of shells to be prized by collectors and children and those seeking souvenirs.

Linen towels printed with shells or gulls, guest soaps masquerading as miniature sea horses, and notepaper packaged in boxes that use small sand dollars as bow ornaments are displayed side by side on the shelves. In one corner nautical prints share shelf space with maps and games and kits relating to the sea, plus a fine assortment of quality books on marine subjects.

There is jewelry too, which includes pendants made

Astoria's West End Mooring Basin, in the heart of the city's waterfront, provides moorage for hundreds of boats in the shadow of the Astoria Bridge, which replaced a ferry system between Oregon and Washington in 1966. The toll bridge is the world's longest continuous truss bridge—1,232 feet.

from minuscule star fish and sand dollars dipped in 24 carat gold—enchanting examples of art masterpieces produced by the ocean.

In an annex room unusual pottery pieces from the kilns of Desdemona Zamettkin and Roland White are offered for sale at prices which seem modest considering the quality of the wares.

Next door is **Reed and Willow Baskets** and **The Kitchen Shop**, recently combined under one manager. Each offers a select assortment of gift items. Basket shops abound these days, but there are some unusuals here—oval mirrors in wicker frames, for instance, and lampshades with a perforated design that shows when the light shines through. An excellent assortment of greeting cards is also displayed here.

The Kitchen Shop features lovely imported enamelware along with special utensils and kitchen accessories. Fine gift foods are available here also.

At the top of the heavy plank stairs is **A Stone's Throw** glittering with fine glass and crystal, much of it imported but also featuring works of local artisans such as the stained glass designed of Kristin Gerde. Especially lovely are paperweights with the appearance of fragile Christmas ornaments from the Alofain-Lundberg studio.

Eye-catching flower paintings by Gregory Briggs of Astoria combine flat white decoupage with painted accents in deep clear blues or reds or yellows, in sizes ranging from $8'' \times 10''$ to $24'' \times 36''$.

Few visitors leave the complex without looking in on the unique carved sea serpent in the lounge of **The Feedstore Restaurant** on the waterfront side of the building. The polished hardwood hand-carved serpent supports a counter 20 feet long on its looped coils. Restaurant and lounge are open 10 a.m. to 10 p.m. for pleasurable dining.

Ye Olde Feedstore Deli at the opposite end of the complex is a treasure trove for the sandwich lover. Gourmet sandwiches bearing intriguing names include such delicacies as

Desdemonia (roast beef, turkey, swiss cheese), **Stormin'
William** (meat loaf and sliced onion), and **King Columbia**
(salmon and cream cheese) all laced with lettuce, tomato, and
sprouts. Or order one custom-made by name: **Biddle** (choice
of 3 cheeses, 3 meats) and **Trees, Cheese, Ocean Breeze** (2
meats, 2 cheeses) plus the trimmings listed above.

Salads are a specialty here along with desserts, including
cheesecake. The Deli pushes Oregon products in their "all
orders to go" food service. They are open 11 a.m. to 7 p.m.,
and make free delivery on orders of $10 or over.

Seafood "Super" Markets

Next door to Pier 11 is the **Ocean Foods Market**, which
specializes in fine foods from the sea. They aren't just kid-
ding when they advertise *fresh* fish; visitors can watch
fishing boats unloading the day's haul with a good possibility
that their subsequent purchases in the sales room may include some of the same. Along with seafood still cool from
the ocean deeps they also sell shrimp and crab cocktails in
their own special sauce, plus smoked, kippered, pickled, and
canned seafood products, and sourdough bread.

Near the entrance to the Astoria toll bridge is
Josephson's Smokehouse. Now in their 60th year in the no-
nonsense box of a building with its advertising painted on the
narrow siding, they merchandise the finest in Scandinavian
delicacies such as sweet-and-sour pickled salmon (from an
old family recipe) and their brine-cured smoked salmon.
Josephson's will custom pack and ship items from their retail
room to any part of the country.

A special eating establishment in this area is worth exploring: **Fiddler's Green Family Pub** serves seafood (featuring
a catch-of-the-day special), steaks, sandwiches, and grog
from an a la carte menu, and throws in extras like darts, and
piano singalongs on Friday and Saturday evenings. Look for
Fiddler's underneath the bridge. It's a place to enjoy the
evening—not to eat and run.

About Town

Astoria is famous for its fine old 19th Century homes—outstanding examples of Italianate, Queen Anne, Victorian, and Gothic architecture. A six-block stretch of Franklin Avenue (700 through 1200 blocks) contains more than a dozen of the elegant mansions; another group clusters in the 1600 block on Grand.

Flavel House epitomizes the Victorian houses which have become landmarks in the city. Built in 1883 by Captain George Flavel, a ship captain/merchant who planned his dream house years ahead of its building, the foundations were laid in a block-square site already lavishly landscaped. It was constructed by a ship's carpenter from San Francisco and has stood the wear and tear of gales from the stormy Columbia River estuary without noticeable damage.

Since 1938 the house has been the property of Clatsop County. The home, much of it preserved as it was when the Flavels resided there, now houses the Clatsop County Historical Society and Museum.

Known far and wide as "the house with the red roof," it served as a landmark for ships entering the Columbia for many years. Now it sits in quiet elegance looking out over the harbor, no longer the center of the city's social activity but the archivist of its past.

The Columbia River Maritime Museum

Astoria, as befits a historic city at the mouth of one of the world's great rivers, boasts the finest all around West Coast maritime museum north of San Francisco. The museum, housed in what was formerly the city hall, is located on the hillside a block and a half above the waterfront, easily recognized by the 25,000 *ton* anchor (from the World War II battleship *Indiana*) which looms like a gargantuan harpoon tip at the south side of the building.

Inside, the halls and rooms are filled with exhibits that chronicle 200 years of the region's maritime history. A marvelous collection of ship models range in size from 3 inches to 10 feet and include a rare large-scale model of the battleship *Oregon*.

A life-size replica of a ship's bridge is a drawing card for adventurous youngsters. The signal unit from the old North Head Light Station centers the lighthouse exhibit and allows visitors a close view of one of the beautiful French lenses which were used in light stations along the northern Pacific Coast.

Flotsam from many a north coast shipwreck has come to rest here, including the carved name plates from the *Peter Iredale* whose wreckage is visible on the beach near Fort Stevens State Park.

Descending the stairway, visitors see hanging in a cove stairwell the 8-foot wheel from the lighthouse tender *Manzanita*, stationed for many years at Tongue Point; its hardwood spokes, inlaid with lighter wood, radiating from a gleaming brass center plate a foot in diameter.

The list seems endless, and the items fascinating. There is no better way to spend an hour or two than to browse through this remarkable compendium of marine artifacts. The continually growing collection threatens to overflow its present quarters before completion of the ultramodern building on the waterfront below the present site which will house the museum, once it is completed.

The Columbia

Star exhibit of the Maritime Museum, the lightship *Columbia* (retired) already rides at anchor near the new location. She was brought around the Horn through the Straits of Magellan in 1907 and began 30 years of service in 1909 at the mouth of the Columbia.

While in service she had a full compliment of 16 crew members—10 or 11 on ship and the other third ashore. The tour of duty was six weeks aboard ship and three weeks off, until the Coast Guard assumed control of the light stations in 1940. With the New Deal regulations in force at that time, the duty schedule was regulated to conform to a 40-hour week for crew members, and for a time the ratio shifted to three weeks off-duty to two weeks on. The ship was converted to steam in 1936, three years before her retirement as a lightship in 1939.

The *Columbia*, now restored to top condition, seems more roomy inside than she appears from without. True, the bunk frames, eight to a room, could only be described as cozy, even without mattresses. But the compact gallery is reminiscent of the kitchens in many modern apartment units, and the leather-covered built-in seats in the ward room provide plenty of sitting space.

Of interest are the wooden mess tables, framed with inch-wide molding with open corners to keep tableware from sliding off during stormy weather while allowing spills to drain away. The white-painted infirmary, barely wide enough to hold a single bunk with raised sides evokes an image of a frightened sailor tossing there during a storm.

But the *Columbia* was good duty according to Chief Petty Officer Mo Mason, who served 24 years with the Coast Guard, and deserves her retirement career as a living history exhibit in her home port.

The small charge of 50¢ per adult and 25¢ for children buys all the time visitors wish to take looking around the ship.

Fees at the museum are $1.50 for adults, 50¢ for students and seniors, and are added to money from memberships, grants, and gifts to keep the project operating.

Both museum and lightship are open daily from 10:30 a.m. to 5:30 p.m. May through October; during winter months, 10:30 a.m. to 4:30 p.m. every day except Mondays.

Astoria Toll Bridge

The graceful bridge which crosses the Columbia River at Astoria is the final link in US Highway 101 which completes the continuous highway system from Canada to Mexico.

Opened in 1966, it is 1,232 feet long—the world's longest truss bridge.

The Astoria Queen
No longer operating

The only sternwheeler cruise boat operating on the Columbia River is berthed at Astoria between Piers Two and Three. *The Astoria Queen* makes regular cruises daily beginning about the end of May and lasting into fall. The moderate rates for this hour and 15 minute cruise around Astoria's waterfront area places it within family budget limits. And children under six are admitted free when accompanied by an adult.

Scenic Flights

An overview of the waterfront is available also. The **Astoria Flight Service** operating out of Clatsop County Airport at Warrenton makes scenic flights along the upper left-hand corner of the state with special rates for two or more persons per trip. They also provide air taxi service.

WARRENTON

Warrenton, the small (2,500 population) town 15 miles downriver from sister city Astoria, is deceptive in appearance and reputaion. It might seem the old town, by-passed by Highway 101 as it cuts across between Seaside and Astoria, had sat out the 80 years since its incorporation without change, and planned to continue doing so in time to come.

Not so. Warrenton has 16 square miles of mostly undeveloped city land—the state's largest "empty" city. Development of modern boat basin facilities has already begun which could boost this "forgotten" town into a prime coastal location.

The moving force behind the development of Warrenton was Daniel Knight Warren, an entrepreneur involved in railroads, lumber mills, cattle raising, banking, and logging. It was Warren who diked the Skipanon River over 100 years ago, using imported Chinese laborers to hand-work the project. From this beginning the growth of Warrenton as the charter boat center of the Columbia River was assured.

The Skipanon River Mooring Basin, built in the mid-fifties by the US Corps of Engineers, is the focus of Warrenton's business area. Fine charter services like **Skipanon Charters** and **Warrenton Deep Sea Charter Service** operate Coast Guard approved boats out of the basin for some of the finest salmon fishing in the world. Commercial seafood processors encourage visitors to come watch the canning and freezing of their products.

Young's Bay Plaza

The area's newest shopping center is located at the intersection of Harbor Drive and Highway 101 between Astoria and Warrenton. The small businesses center around a supermarket and a drugstore.

Among them is a branch of Astoria's famous **Home Bakery**, which features breads, cakes, and pastries from old-world recipes that have been the bakery's pride since its founding in 1910 by the father of the present owner. They specialize in a large variety of Scandinavian breads using no preservatives.

Also located here is **Admiral House**, one of the region's newest and better restaurants. The family dinner house features a Sunday Champagne Breakfast Buffet, plus daily specials for both lunch and dinner in addition to the regular menu. The attractive surroundings highlighted by cedar paneling and planter box dividers include a distinctive metal sculpture as a room separater.

Families are welcomed here, of course; reservations are available. There is plenty of parking for campers and RVs. The prices for excellent service and good food are in the moderate range.

A mile or so down on East Harbor Drive is **The Buccaneer Deli**, an all around delight. In addition to a fine assortment of imported and domestic cheeses, plus deli meats, wine, and beer, the Buccaneer features sandwiches and orders to go. A daily treat is their 3:30-4:30 p.m. dessert and coffee hour. You'll have to get up early to catch the Buccaneer asleep on the job: opening hour during fishing season is a cool 4 a.m.

Two fine swimming areas at Coffenbury Lake in Fort Stevens State Park are equipped with bath houses and log booms for the convenience of those enjoying its sandy beaches. A boat launching ramp at the north end is an added attraction for enthusiasts who come for the excellent trout and perch fishing. A 2½-mile hiking trail encircles the lake itself, and more trails wind through the park. A large picnic area borders the lake, and facilities at the adjacent campground include 225 trailer sites with utility hookups, 120 improved campsites, and 260 tent sites.

Fort Stevens State Park

The star attraction of the region is Fort Stevens, the country's most westerly military installation from the Civil War through the end of World War II. The original earthworks, begun by Union soldiers who feared Confederate ships might come into the Columbia River, were completed the *day before* General Lee signed the surrender papers at Appomattox on April 4, 1865.

Decommissioned in 1947, after a long and honorable career, Fort Stevens was retired at the height of its fame—the only military target in the continental United States to be attacked during World War II—the first indeed since the War of 1812.

The attack came on June 22, 1942, while the country was still trying to recover from the psychological trauma of the attack on Pearl Harbor which decimated our South Pacific fleet and left our defenses vulnerable to the powerful Japanese navy. It started about 10:30 p.m. while most men at Battery Russell, the gun emplacement under attack, were asleep. The Japanese submarine *I-25* fired 17 rounds of shells, one coming within 300 yards of the battery. Unsure of the source of the attack, officers did not order the guns fired in retaliation, although soldiers were sent to the beach in anticipation of an enemy landing craft operation.

Daily walking tours of the rusting iron installations still at Fort Stevens Military Reservation are conducted starting in June. Park rangers have been reconstructing the remaining buildings and are on hand to answer questions.

The historical center for the Fort is housed in the former War Games building, with exhibits, relics, and interpretive displays about the historic Fort.

Also within the Fort Stevens State Park is the wreckage of the *Peter Iredale*, a British ship grounded in 1907 during a storm while on its way from Australia to Portland to take on a load of wheat. The skeleton of the 287-foot four-masted sailing ship, driven into the "shelving sands" by a strong current, remains there, slowly disintegrating, too deeply embedded to be moved.

Annual Events

The Scandinavian Midsummer Festival—a week-end celebration of the area's ethnic heritage in mid-June.
The Astoria Regatta—late August.

SEASIDE

Seaside is a coastal resort town—Oregon's largest—designed for that role by its founder, transportation king Ben Holladay, who covered the West with railroads and stage coaches, and established shipping routes to supplement them.

In 1871 Holladay built a lavish seaside hotel in the area first settled by a Scot, Alexander Latty, a ship's captain with the Hudson Bay Company, and Solomon Smith, a teacher at Fort Vancouver. Attractive extras for the recreation minded patron of *Seaside House* included a race track and the horses to run, and a wild animal zoo. These, plus the natural beauty of the golden beach, insured its immediate popularity. The colorful Holladay, as much a showman as P.T. Barnum, required his fleet of coastal steamers to salute the flag which flew from the Seaside House's rooftop flagstaff with cannon fire each time they passed.

Replacement of the old boardwalk along Seaside's ocean front in the early 1920's established the city once and for all as an ocean resort in the grand manner, and it became known as the Coastal Capital of Oregon. Today the fine old hotels and residences fronted by the Prom are being elbowed aside by modern resorts whose glittering glass and steel tend to overpower the fading glory of the genteel originals.

Annual Events

The approach to the famous **Turnaround**—the official end point of the Lewis and Clark Trail—is somehow diminished by the crowded street and limited parking. But it's there, and just beyond lies the beautiful stretch of sandy beach which has always been Seaside's main charm. Over the years it has served as the stage for several annual events which draw visitors by the thousands to the tiny city.

The **Trail's End Marathon**, held each year in February, has grown a thousandfold in the 10 years of its existence. Organized to bring tourists to the resort town during the off-season, it has succeeded far beyond the goals of the contest's developers. The race begins at the Turnaround overlooking the beach, when the more than 2,000 entrants—kindergartners to senior citizens—line up for the beginning of the 26-mile endurance contest. Only about three-fourths of the contestants finish the race, but all entrants receive a Trail's End T-shirt, and spectators line the course by the hundreds to cheer them on.

In mid-July the emphasis is on quality rather than quantity as the **Miss America Pageant** turns the spotlight on Oregon's loveliest young women, who vie for a chance to represent the state in the national contest at Atlantic City. Traditionally the contestants appear on the famous beach to display their charms and have their pictures taken in the latest style (but always one-piece) bathing suits.

In August the runners again take over the beach for **The Seaside Beach Run**, a seven-mile course which keeps them slogging through sand from start to finish. The race, which began with 100 contestants 15 years ago, now tops 800 entrants, with spectators more than doubling the influx of visitors to the area for the event.

Each year Seaside becomes more what it is. The new modern convention center, which can handle groups of 2,000, clinches the town's position as one of the largest, most attractive resort towns on the Northwest coast.

Some Special Shops

The Honey Wind Herb Farm deals in organically grown herbs and is open every afternoon at its location on North Highway 101.

Britannia Antiques in the same area offers both American and European furniture, plus brass, copper, and Depression glass.

At the south end of Holladay coming into town is **The Prom Bike Shop** recognizable by the old-fashioned bicycles with huge front wheels silhouetted against spanking white buildings. This is a full service shop: rent a bike, have a tire fixed, or buy a new one here.

Joantiques, also on South Holladay, has dolls, collectables, and conventional antiques.

No trip to Seaside is complete without a visit to **Harrison's Bakery** on Broadway close downtown. Founded in 1914, the bakery produces around a thousand loaves of special recipe breads—over 35 varieties—a day in addition to cookies, pastries, and other goodies all made from scratch using pure natural ingredients with no preservatives. Harrison's products taste the way we all remember "homemade."

The Seaside Turnaround at the end of Broadway is a traditional gathering place. Viewed from the balcony of the Seasider Hotel, it looks much the same as it did in the days of excursion trains and early motor cars.

The Lunch Basket Deli on Broadway features domestic and imported wines; Oregon jams, jelly, honey; imported cheeses, and over 20 varieties of imported beer; plus deli goods and lunches.

A "must" stop is **Fenton's Farmers Market** on Highway 101 north of Seaside. Allen and Ellen Fenton have spent the last 14 years building this thriving market/garden shop.

The market section in the older building has an open front hedged by large buckets of superior cut flowers whose colors glow even on the rainiest day. In the open-air section directly behind them, top quality fruits and vegetables add their own bold colors: red-purple eggplants gleam alongside emerald green peppers the size of grapefruit, the rich jewel tones enhancing each other. Golden squash, bright red radishes, sea-green celery all add to the montage of produce as colorful as the illustrations in a deluxe seed catalog. Skin tones of potatoes shade from near-white to red to dusky brown in the wooden crates which serve as bins from which customers pick and choose produce piece by piece. Prices are printed with felt-tip pens on brown paper sacks stapled to walls or racks.

It's strictly self-serve at Fenton's. Brown eggs are the most popular item, stored in an old-fashioned box refrigerator. Oregon honey is dispensed from a large container near the central counter built from 18-inch square driftwood timbers from an old shipwreck.

There are gift items too, among them chain-saw totem-type masks produced by a local craftsman.

The garden shop is in a new section of the establishment designed and built by an English architect, a tourist who visited in its early days and became a friend of the Fentons. Plank walls in design patterns are hung with pages from old newspapers displayed behind glass panels. One front page of *The Oregonian* is dated October 24th, 1898, and features, in addition to the standard patent medicine advertisements typical of the time, news with miniscule headlines which report "Indian Trouble is Brewing." Ceiling rafters form a rectangular lattice effect beneath translucent roof panels.

The building is heated throughout by large iron drum-type stoves; the Fentons cut and split their own firewood.

The garden showroom is flanked on both sides by outdoor patio areas in which nursery plants and trees are displayed as part of the landscaping. From any point, inside or out, one views charming vistas of plants, hangings, and wall sections. The front patio roof is supported by a row of cedar telephone poles.

Highlight of the year for the Fentons is the week before Memorial Day, when a huge central room behind the main market section is banked ceiling high on all four walls with cannisters of fresh flowers. People come from all over the Northwest Coast to select memorial floral tributes from among the quality flowers on display.

Fenton's is open every day, 9 a.m. to 6 p.m.

Easy to Find Eateries

For seafood try **The Seasider** near The Turnaround, or **Norma's**, 182 Broadway.

International menus are offered at **Kan's**, 42 years in the same location (Chinese), and **Finnegan & Co.** (Continental) both on Broadway; and at **Pizza Palace** (Italian) on Highway 101 North.

The **Broadway Cafe** (homemade pies) and **The Wagoneer** (western style), both on Broadway, are good breakfast and lunch places.

Year-Around Attractions

The 43-year-old **Seaside Aquarium** two blocks north of The Turnaround on the Prom is noted for its growing family of harbor seals. The aquarium has pioneered in breeding these animals, and "youngsters" from one to 99 are entranced by their amusing performances. The outstanding assortment of marine life exhibits—up to 1,500 varieties—includes rare sea turtles and wolf fish, moray eels and leopard sharks plus an octopus.

A few blocks south of The Turnaround, just below the

Prom in a small courtyard boxed in by residences, is the replica of the **Lewis and Clark Salt Cairn**, where a small detachment of men from the historic expedition spent the better part of two months making salt the winter of 1806.

The low rock cairn is constructed to specifications found in the expedition diaries and mounds to a flattened top to hold small "kittles" like the ones in which three to four quarts of salt were produced daily while the project was in operation.

Ultimately four bushels were obtained, which provided a "most agreeable addition" to the limited diets of the men at Fort Clatsop 14 miles to the north. The 12 gallons packed in small kegs and laid by for the return voyage proved valuable as trade goods as well as for personal use on game, roots, fish, and roast dog which made up the menu during the trip home.

The cairn has been reconstructed on the exact site of the original, established through the memory of Jenny Mishel, a woman of the Clatsop tribe whose father had shown her the spot when she was a child.

The monument, maintained in its natural state as nearly as fences, plaques, and walkways will allow, helps to illuminate a minor facet of one of the most significant voyages of exploration in the history of the United States.

The Raintree Gift and Garden Center at the southern end of Seaside on Highway 101 was originally conceived as a gift shop that would carry a few houseplants by owners Dennis and Mary Lee Saulsbury. By the end of their first season, they found the plants were the main attraction, and they now specialize in unusual and hard to find plantings. Available here are orange and lemon trees, lilacs (difficult to locate these days), and one of the most extensive selections of succulents along the coast. An outstanding example is the purple rose tree, a native of the Canary Islands, whose long stems end in 4-inch "blossoms" of flat-leaf rosettes which turn a deep purple as the tree "blooms."

The service area has just about any possible tool or supplies for gardeners. The Saulsburys mean it when they advertise, "We'll be happy to cultivate your green thumb."

Their clients come from all over the country, with a sprinkling of foreign visitors. One devoted patron voiced the sentiments of their many repeat customers when she said, "I wouldn't dream of leaving Seaside without stopping at the Raintree!"

Ecola State Park adjacent to Cannon Beach is known for the spectacular coastal scenery within its borders. Plentiful picnic sites (with camp stoves) are available for those wishing to take advantage of the excellent swimming, hiking, fishing, and beachcombing. It was to this area that Captain Lewis brought Sacajawea to show her the beached whale during the winter the expedition spent at Fort Clatsop.

CANNON BEACH

The rusty cannon for which Cannon Beach is named, mounted near the north end of the loop road which leads from the highway to the resort village, was washed ashore from the wreckage of the United States Schooner *Shark* in 1846. But that symbol of military might is somehow out of tone with the charm of the beach and the town which borders it.

Famed **Haystack Rock**, the world's third largest coastal monolith, is the landmark which centers the nine-mile long beach fronting this cluster of shops, restaurants, and natural recreational accommodations for vacationers and tourists. Created over the ages by pounding tides which shaped it from mountains long since turned to sand, the 235-foot rock is still undergoing change. Since the turn of the century two of its small side "needles" have been devoured by the sea, leaving two to go.

The tidepools at the base of the rock become a living museum at low tide, with ever-changing exhibits of crabs, mussels, starfish, and anemones. The rock itself is a national bird sanctuary offering visitors opportunities to observe the marine fowl which live there.

The rock was lighted at night during a short period several years ago, but environmentalists forced the removal of the floodlights.

Some Special Shops

Resort towns tend to reflect the quality of their shops, which represent a large part of the attraction for the tourists and vacationers who are necessary for their survival. In Cannon Beach the stress is on quality, and there are more than enough special shops and galleries there to support the emphasis.

Ingle-Nook is representative of the fine show-and-sell shops established by artisans and craftspeople on the Oregon Coast. Weavers Carolyn Locke and Louise Lindsey bring their talents in other fields of art to bear in producing the intricate pieces of artistic weaving they create, exhibit, and market in their showroom in Sandpiper Square. Natural fiber supplies

Tide pools at the base of Haystack Rock (Cannon Beach) hold a fascinating group of intertidal animals. This is a protected area, however, so living creatures may not be taken there.

and accessories for knitters and weavers are carried also, plus some imported goods.

Visitors are welcome to watch the artists at work at their looms or to browse the fine selection of their works on exhibit. They also accept custom orders for the hangings, shawls, and other items they create.

Also recommended: **Renaissance Gallery** showing both originals and reproductions of fine paintings; **Fair Winds** which specializes in marine oils and watercolors, and quality nautical artifacts—both on North Hemlock Street. **Otter Woods Pottery** on East Second produces imaginative utilitarian and decorative pottery items.

Gift shops with colorful names abound: **The Puffin** (myrtlewood); **Thistledown** (bellows, boxes, bangles, and bells); **The Bird and Bead** (jewelry, beads, and shells) to name a few.

Specialty shops stand shoulder to shoulder along the beach loop road: **American Dream Quilts** (quilts); **Grandma Ruthie's** (creative fabric items); **Once Upon a Breeze** (kites); and **The Wine Shack** (domestic and imported).

Not easily passed by is **The Ice Creamery**. Now in its third year, the small shop reflects proprietor Jim Osburn's personal taste in art. The walls behind the ice cream case are hung with his private collection of paintings and drawings by local artists.

The ice cream counter is set up behind two decorative carved wooden pillars, part of the original old store building, now painted gold. Ice cream dispensed is from the Alpenrose Dairies near Portland.

His parents, Will and Judy Osburn, operate a grocery store and delicatessen next door—**The Gourmet Food Store for Thrifty Gourmets**—which sells custom made sandwiches and homemade take-outs. Both of these are fun places to shop.

Bruce's Candy Kitchen is the granddaddy of Cannon Beach shops. It looks rather like a pink and white candy box from the street. Inside the glass candy counters which display the homemade chocolates and salt-water taffy are topped with big glass jars filled with licorice whips, jelly beans, and other familiar goodies.

Crowding the rest of the shop are racks and trays and shelves of souvenirs and novelties.

The Cannon Beach Bakery, famous for its haystack bread, is also a veteran among the array of shops.

The round building across the street from Bruce's Candy Kitchen houses **Pat's Baskets and Coffees**. The shop carries an exceptional assortment of woven containers, from party cups to outsized hampers and trays, plus one of the largest selections of wall baskets in the Northwest.

The coffee section is stocked with fine coffees and tea and displays of quality gift servers and accessories, including espresso and cappuccino makers.

The owner also sells coffee and tea by the cup and provides small tables for customers who want to try them.

The complex of red buildings with the white gingerbread trim as travelers come into Cannon Beach from the north look like something out of Walt Disney—but they aren't. This is the **Cannon Beach Conference Center**, founded in 1944 by the Reverend Archie McNeil and his wife Evangeline as a non-denominational Christian center in an old log hotel with a few cabins to accommodate participants.

Today the modern facility can house 300 guests and feed 400. The year-round center includes six large motel units, a dining room, a bakery, and a snack bar, plus a bookstore. Non-credit Bible classes are offered through the school year, with lectures, workshops, and retreats held in the summer. The present operators are the daughters of the founders and their husbands.

Annual Events

Haystack Rock is the namesake for the **Haystack Summer Workshops** offered annually through Portland State University. Designed to coordinate with family vacations, the program offers continuing workshops in music, art, photography, fine crafts, and creative writing, led by professionals in their fields.

Cannon Beach retains an atmosphere of small-town charm which holds through the onslaught of hundreds of contestants plus thousands of spectators who show up every year for the **Cannon Beach Sand Sculpture Contest**. What began as a children's activity 16 years ago now includes adults— limited to 100 teams—and prizes awarded in a number of special categories.

The contest starts at 7 a.m. Contestants have three hours in which to create their imaginative masterpieces, which run the gamut from autos to giants to sandcastles to zebras and includes almost anything in between. Spectators receive equal time for viewing and snapping pictures between 10 a.m. when the judging starts and 1 p.m. when the tides sweep them away in a spectacular ending to the event held each year between late June and mid-July.

The Cape Meares Lighthouse just south of Tillamook Bay along the Netarts-Oceanside loop, is one of the most picturesque of the Oregon coast. When built in 1890, it was intended for the point that is presently called Cape Lookout. Due to a survey mixup which switched the names, the lighthouse was built on the former Cape Lookout, published on maps as Cape Meares (which it has remained). Now unmanned, it remains a favorite of visitors.

The Lighthouses

Oregon's six lighthouses seem fragile, toylike, to be standing guard along a primitive coastline carved by an ocean reaching halfway around the globe. But titanic waves generated by 6,000 miles of empty seas, colliding with the continent's edge in continuous assault, make them necessary. A shoreline sculpted from prehistoric mountains made construction of these isolated towers, built during the last half of the 19th century, as dangerous as navigation of the treacherous off-shore waters which imperiled Captain Cook's ship *Resolution* during his exploration of the Pacific coast one hundred years earlier.

The first lighthouse on the 350-mile long coast, the **Umpqua River Light Station** 20 miles north of Coos Bay, was built in 1857, but within four years it had fallen into the sea, undermined by erosion of the dunes on which it was built. For the next nine years ships in adjacent coastal waters reverted to navigation by visual landmarks such as the white shell mounds accumulated during Indian ceremonies over the years which were visible at great distances from the sea.

In 1866 **Cape Gregory Lighthouse** was erected near the entrance to Coos Bay, but the eight-sided building with a frame of wrought iron had to be moved within a few years because the sea, eating into the connecting rock, had formed a channel between the lighthouse and the mainland. It was replaced by a second tower closer to the shore, which ultimately had to be moved for the same reason as its predecessor.

The present facility was renamed **Cape Arago Lighthouse** after the headland several miles to the south. It is still

separated by a sea channel, tied now to the mainland by a
footbridge built after the basket on a cable, which ferried
early light keepers and supplies to their station, dumped one
man onto the rock below. The station's 110,000 candlepower
light is identified by a distinctive relay of three flashes at
20-second intervals. The lighthouse is located on Coast
Guard property, and personnel residing there maintain the
light, fog signal, and radio beacon which make up the
light station.

In 1868 the original **Yaquina Head Light Station** was raised
on the north side of the Yaquina Bay entrance. Replaced six
years later at another site, the first building is now maintained
as a historic exhibit by the Oregon State Parks system. It is
open to the public from mid-May to Labor Day, furnished in
the style of its origin. Local legend has inhabited the old tower
with the ghost of a former keeper's wife who is said to walk
the empty halls now and then. The tower itself is indicated as
a day mark on current marine charts.

Two years later a lighthouse was built on Cape Blanco,
originally Cape Orford. Heavy trees were cleared from the
face of the Cape to make a place for the 59-foot white tower
and separate keeper's house nearby. Bricks for the buildings
were manufactured in the area from local clay. The white
light of the **Cape Blanco Lighthouse** is projected through a
Fresnel system French lens which transforms a 1,000 watt
lightbulb into a distinctive pattern of flashes which skippers
can identify more than 20 miles out to sea. The mechanical
light replaces burned out bulbs automatically, assuring continuous production of the 300,000 candlepower beam. At 250
feet above sea level, Cape Blanco's light is Oregon's highest
as well as the farthest south and west. With resident
keepers, it is the only Oregon light station which maintains
regular, although limited, visiting hours.

The present **Yaquina Head Light Station** was built four
miles north of the entrance to Yaquina Bay on 1,935 acres of
reserve land authorized in 1866 by President Andrew John-
son. Supplies for construction of the 96-foot cone-shaped

tower were hoisted up the cliff face by windlass. The building was completed in August of 1873—but at the wrong site! The station had been designated for Otter Crest, several miles to the north. Automated in 1966, the 110,000 candlepower light projects through the original lens manufactured in Paris in 1868. The signal, a sequence of two white flashes every 20 seconds, shows 162 feet above the water for a range of 50 miles. The station is open for inspection on special occasions only.

The installation of **Tillamook Rock Light**, begun in 1879 on a massive rock a mile offshore and 20 miles south of the mouth of the Columbia River, has the most dramatic history of Oregon's light stations. The exposed site, barely 200 feet above tideline, could serve as a substitute location for "The Exorcist."

The construction crew and materials were transported to the dangerous setting by breeches buoy, and the top of the rock was leveled by blasting crews before work could start on the stone building. Basalt rocks shaped to precision fit at an inland quarry were shipped to the rock by lighthouse tender. The workmen labored under impossible conditions, persistently threatened by heavy seas pounding over the site.

The light station was completed in 1881, after 18 months of arduous labor (including six months' delay due to storm damage which partially destroyed the project) at a cost of one life and $125,000. But the troubles were just beginning. Keepers were at the mercy of a merciless ocean which often sent boulders crashing through walls and into the light itself.

Ships trying to enter the Columbia River were dependent upon the Tillamook Rock Light, the only navigational signal north of Cape Disappointment, for a safe entry into the river's mouth. The 76-year-old light was maintained at a prohibitive cost until September of 1957, when it was replaced by an automated signal and the original installations were abandoned.

It has subsequently passed through the hands of a series of private buyers. NO TRESPASSING signs keep visitors from landing at the rock, but it is visible from Tillamook Head—a disintegrating monument to the men who challenged the destructive power of the Pacific Ocean to install the beacon.

In 1890 the small **Cape Meares Lighthouse** was established near Tillamook Bay. Authorized for construction on Cape Lookout 10 miles farther south, the materials were delivered to the wrong site in the roadless wilderness. The installation was subsequently legalized by a special congressional bill during the term of President Benjamin Harrison. The manned lighthouse was replaced by an automated station in 1963—a 17-foot facility 232 feet atop the Cape,

A familiar sight on Oregon beaches is a lonely lighthouse materializing against the shoreline as early morning mists are chased away by the sun.

In 1894, some 33 years after the first lighthouse on the Umpqua River fell into the sea, the second **Umpqua River Lighthouse** was built on a safer, higher spot at the same location. The white tower 165 feet above sea level houses the only red/white flashing signal on the Oregon coast. With candlepower of 400,000 for the white light and 200,000 for the red, the signal alternates two white flashes with one red flash every 15 seconds. The light station is operated by the Umpqua River Lifeboat Station.

Also in 1894, the **Heceta Head Lighthouse** was built on the coast between Florence and Yachats, 28 miles north of the first station on the Umpqua. Materials for the 56-foot tower were shipped from San Francisco, then hauled in wagons along the beach and over the mountain to the setting. The light stands 205 feet high on the rocky headland, its 1,500,000 candlepower beam flashing a steady white light. The station is manned by resident light keepers.

Although only Cape Blanco Lighthouse maintains visiting hours as such, it is sometimes possible to obtain permission to visit light stations by contacting the Coast Guard units at Cape Arago, Yaquina Head, and on the Umpqua River. And whether inspected close up or from vantage points along the coast, there is an atmosphere of romance and adventure about the sturdy outpost towers scattered along the rocky coastline which seems to linger from another era that has all but disappeared from our lives today.

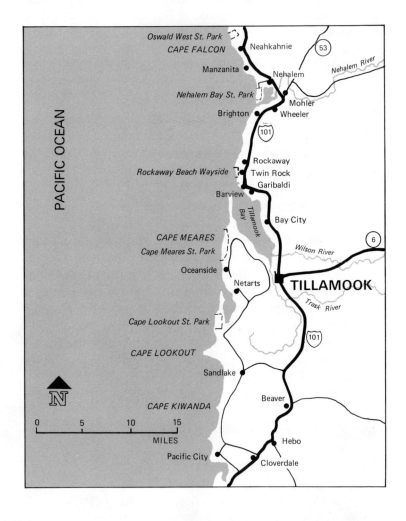

Oswald West St. Park
CAPE FALCON
Neahkahnie
53
Nehalem River
Manzanita
Nehalem
Mohler
Nehalem Bay St. Park
Wheeler
Brighton
101
PACIFIC OCEAN
Rockaway
Rockaway Beach Wayside
Twin Rock
Garibaldi
Barview
Tillamook Bay
Bay City
CAPE MEARES
Cape Meares St. Park
Wilson River
6
Oceanside
Netarts
TILLAMOOK
Trask River
Cape Lookout St. Park
CAPE LOOKOUT
101
Sandlake
N
Beaver
CAPE KIWANDA
0   5   10   15
MILES
Hebo
Pacific City
Cloverdale

Tillamook
Nehalem

TILLAMOOK COUNTY

The Tillamook County Beach is an area for those who want coastal adventure without tourist crowds.

Pacific City, south of the town of Tillamook, is small with limited tourist facilities. But it is home to the fleet of dory fishermen who gather to launch through the milder surf in the shelter of Cape Kiwanda. Fishing charters are available from several dorymen. Customers experience a showery ride from the beach through the surf. Salmon and bottom fish are most frequently caught. The return is a thrilling ride through the breakers to a skidding stop on the sandy beach. To arrange a charter trip, contact the dorymen through Sears Sporting Goods; or watch for such dories as *Pappa's Toy*.

Or, those with scuba training can dive for scallops and ling cod on the offshore reefs and pinnacles that reach up to within 30 feet of the surface. Waters are usually clear, and scallops are always abundant—if you can spot them in their seaweed camouflage. What a place to combine adventures—under the sea and boating through the surf!

One need not participate in the thrills. For a spectator approach, simply watch the commercial fishermen and sports dories as they come and go through the breakers, something that requires skill in picking the right time and right waves to dash through. (They occasionally get dumped.) Or, you can sit or lie on the sand and watch the hang-glider enthusiasts as they sail their colorful crafts from the heights of the cape.

There is an excitement at Pacific City for those who seek it, and peace for those who wish to stroll the uncrowded sandy beach along the sandspit that separates the Nestucca River from the sea. There are five miles of beach between Cape Kiwanda and the mouth of the river, much of it undeveloped.

Also south of Tillamook are the communities of **Netarts** and **Oceanside**. Netarts is situated on the bay of the same name, a body of water that is unusual by being a closed estuary (no river flows into it) and thus having a high salinity. Clams, crabs, and bottom fish are abundant. The sandy peninsula that extends between the bay and the Pacific Ocean holds a fascinating archaeological site, the location of a deserted Indian village. It also provides miles of uninterrupted beach-combing.

Nearby, Oceanside boasts a sandy beach that erodes each winter to a gravelly layer that contains numerous agates. The picturesque pedestrian tunnel hewn through the rock point at the north end of Oceanside has recently been plagued by slides. Efforts are underway to correct the situation. Presently, access to seashells and jade-like green rocks on the beach beyond is limited to low tide.

Late February each year the two communities join together and present a Beachcomber Fair that features displays of glass floats and driftwood, talks by authors of ocean-related books, and homemade pastries.

The town of **Tillamook** is the county seat and largest community of the area. Located away from the ocean, at the back of a large bay fed by the Miama, Kilchis, Wilson, Trask, and Tillamook rivers, it features shopping facilities and the famous Tillamook Cheese Factory. In Oregon's pioneer era it was isolated from the rest of the territory, and was seldom visited by traders. The settlers finally built their own schooner in 1854, naming it the *Morning Star*. A full-scale seaworthy replica of the ship rests in front of the Tillamook Cheese Factory.

Although access for fishing and clamming is available throughout Tillamook Bay, the most action takes place from the boat basin at **Garibaldi** on the northern edge of the estuary. Garibaldi has close access to the channel leading charter boats out to sea, launching and moorage facilities for private boats, and tourist facilities. Three restaurants with good food and average prices—Joe's Charter Cafe, The Troller, and The Bay Side—are located at the boat basin. Scuba divers find spearfishing around nearby rocks and on the north jetty of the Tillamook Bay entrance.

Sightseeing is best on the south side of the bay, toward Cape Meares. There, the ocean has made inroads into the land, leaving huge, gray tree trunks and gnarled roots upon the beach. Stretching northward from this eroded area is the narrow peninsula that separates Tillamook Bay from the Pacific. This peninsula once held the community of Bayocean—which the ocean claimed.

Just north of Garibaldi are some of Tillamook County's most populous tourist beaches—Twin rocks, Rockaway, and Manhattan Beach (even the name suggests lots of people). Motels and restaurants dot these communities, though most of the space is taken by homes of those who have come to enjoy the sandy beaches. The tone is quiet, however, as these are mostly older cottages and older motels—for older, more sedate occupants.

While the Tillamook Bay is an extensive one, fed by five coastal rivers, and spreads northward to its link with the sea, neighboring **Nehalem Bay** is fed by a single river, the Nehalem. However, that river drains a stretch of land reaching two thirds of the way to Portland, beginning just 12 miles from the Columbia River. The Nehalem estuary is narrower and outlets to the south—close to the Tillamook mouth. Despite its size, it is filled with history and legend. Predominant is the legend of the treasure of Neahkahnie Mountain, and it is true that a mysterious English vessel came to rest in the bay some time around the 1790's. Lesser treasures, old bottles and relics from ships, are still to be found by scuba divers working several areas of Nehalem Bay.

Along the shore of the bay are the quiet communities of **Wheeler**, considerably diminished from the days of the tidewater sawmills and lumber schooners, and **Nehalem**. A cluster of rebuilt shops in Nehalem have brought new vitality to the town. This active little community also features a canoe race in May and an art festival in July.

Nehalem is a fascinating community to stop and shop in, and the Nehalem Bay has good fishing, crabbing, and clam digging.

West of Nehalem, at the beach, is **Manzanita**. It still retains some of the quiet charm but is rapidly growing. A few motels and two restaurants are found at Manzanita, but the community is mostly private homes and summer cottages.

Adjoining Manzanita, on the ashpit, is a State Park with picnic facilities, camping and trailer sites, a boat ramp, and access to both Nehalem Bay and the ocean beach.

James Seeley White

James Seeley White of Portland, Oregon is the author of "Seashells of the Pacific Northwest", "Diving for Northwest Relics", and "The Hedden's Store Handbook."

NEHALEM

At Manzanita Junction Highway 101 makes a turn inland, to begin a 25-mile drive which loops around Nehalem and Tillamook Bays and includes some of the most delightful areas on the north coast.

Nehalem at the north end of the drive is a novelist's love of a fishing village. There is a dreamlike quality to the town overlooking its tranquil bay, as an old woman sits in her rocking chair on a homestead porch recalling the impatient yearnings of youth while relishing the comforts achieved through

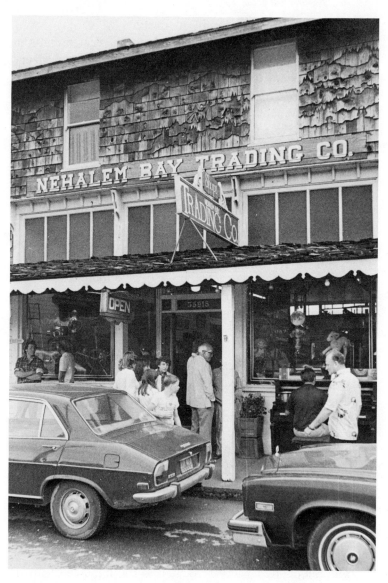

Rebuilt stores like the Nehalem Bay Trading Company offer excellent shopping for gifts, antiques, and nautical relics in the town of Nehalem. A piano player entertains visitors during the arts festival.

the compromises demanded by maturity.

And there is much tangible evidence of past dreams in Nehalem, the "antique center of the Oregon coast." Every other shop seems to offer pretested merchandise to tempt those who love heritage furnishings and glass and china and...you name it. It's all here in Nehalem.

Old and New

Rain Barrel Antiques, Nehalem Bay Trading Company, Betty's This and That, and others all sell antiques *plus*, and are all located within shouting distance of each other in the part of the town where the highway scoots down the hill and makes an abrupt turn in the middle of the two-block long "city center."

But along with vintage treasures can be found the works of artisans who are creating tomorrow's heirlooms. Goldsmith Christopher Shepherd designs and executes the unique jewelry displayed in his cases: delicate rings in turn-of-the-century styles as well as bold free-form modern pieces. A tiny gold pine cone pendant lies next to large medallions. These one-of-a-kind pieces, beautifully wearable, are also to be valued as investments.

But the jewelry is only the beginning. During the three years his shop has been in operation, Christopher Shepherd has attracted a coterie of fine artists and craftspeople whose imaginative works are shown for sale at the **Shepherd Gallery**: the metal sculpture of Sam Gendusa; cuddly soft animals by *Stuff It*; kites by *White Bird*, among others. Pottery by several artists is unique in color and design, especially that from *Barlow* works, simple basic forms set off by inlaid patterns in contrasting tones to create a distinctive effect.

The Shepherd Gallery is located at the hill side of town, Highway 101 at 9th Street.

The Bookworm is worth browsing. Its shelves hold games as well as a wide selection of books, including late editions.

The **Riverboat Inn**, right downtown, and the **Hungry**

Whale Drive-In (at the Nehalem Bay Trailer and Camping Resort) provide eating accommodations in Nehalem. For brownbaggers, a small shaded lookout in the "corner" area holds a park bench where visitors can view the bay while lunching.

Free boat launchings and private moorings are a convenience for fishers and boaters who favor the quiet river bay over more crowded sites.

Most travelers will leave Nehalem's serene setting with regret.

The Tillamook County Cheese, Food, and Wine Tour

Anchor for the trip is the **Nehalem Bay Winery**, the only winery on the Oregon/Washington coast. Remodeled from a former Mohler Creamery Association cheese factory, it is located on Mohler Road just south of Nehalem. Pat and Adrienne McCoy, Nehalem Bay's owners, produce several varietal grape wines plus an assortment of fruit and berry wines made from premium Northwest products.

Visitors are encouraged to browse through the winery on self-guided tours and are welcomed in the handsome tasting room with its driftwood bar for samples of Nehalem Bay products. **Nehalem Bay Winery** is open 10 a.m.-5 p.m. June through Labor Day, noon to 5 p.m. the rest of the year except for major holidays.

At Garibaldi, next stop on the tour, a jackpot of seafood plants awaits the tourist. **Phil & Joe's Crab Company**, open every day 9 a.m.-5 p.m. (later hours in summer) for processing fresh seafood, is easy to spot on Highway 101 coming into town. The other two are neighbors at Fisherman's Wharf near the town's center. **Smith's Pacific Shrimp Company** has a large viewing room for observing the processing of their wares; their sales room is open April through mid-October, 9 a.m.-5 p.m. **The Olson Oyster Company** offers plant tours where visitors can watch the preparation of oysters for marketing. Their sales room is in operation 9 a.m.-5 p.m. April through mid-September.

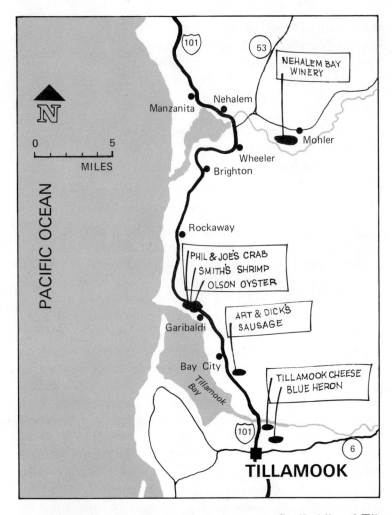

At Bay City, roughly halfway between Garibaldi and Tillamook, **Art & Dick's Sausage Company**, noted up and down the coast for their fine smoked meats, especially the pepper bacon, is open seven days a week the year around and is easy to locate driving through the town.

The tour ends at Tillamook with the cheese processing plants, the oldest and the newest of the companies that make up the tour.

The **Morning Star II** is a full-scale replica of the schooner built in 1854 by settlers of the isolated Tillamook Bay area to provide a means of marketing their products, since they were usually by-passed by coastal traders. It is on display near the entrance to the Tillamook Cheese Factory, whose quality products are shipped throughout the world.

Tillamook County Creamery, the largest cheese processing plant in the world, is open daily through the week, 9 a.m.-5 p.m. Famed around the country for its Tillamook cheddar, the plant has a large glass-walled viewing room where the half-million visitors a year who come to the plant may observe the steps in cheese making and receive a slide-and-tape presentation of supplemental information on the Tillamook dairy products.

The dairy bar and tasting room, featuring the company's superlative ice cream as well as cheese, is also open daily, and sales personnel will wrap and mail gift packs upon request.

The huge factory is easily located from the highway by the near life-size replica of the *Morning Star* in the front courtyard.

Newest of the companies is **Blue Heron French Cheese Factory** at the south end of town. Just a year old, the tasting room is open daily for visitors to sample imported cheeses and the French-style breakfast cheese which is manufactured there. The retail room also carries imported coffees, specialty foods, and Blue Heron T-shirts. One corner is countered off as a wine-tasting room where selected wine from Nehalem Bay Winery can be sampled.

The operation is housed in a former dairy barn now painted white with the Blue Heron logo larger than life on each of the gable ends, making it easy to identify driving by in spite of its being back off the road behind other buildings.

The cheese, food, and wine tasting tour offers an excellent opportunity to sample Oregon products which have gained a well-deserved reputation for quality.

Special Dining

Before leaving Tillamook take time to visit **The Victory House** restaurant in the city's center. House specialties plus fine service will make visitors want to return. Meals include homemade bread warm from the oven and homemade wild blackberry jam. 'Nuff said!

Pacific City is home of the adventurous dory fleet. Dr. James McMillan, owner of **Salty**, is an ardent scuba diver as well as fisherman. When the swells run three feet or less in height, as on this day, the sea is quiet enough to dive on the off-shore reef.

Nostalgia

Sea Life at Rockaway is a nostalgia center for those who can remember pre-World War II visits to the Oregon coast. It's crowded (all good souvenir shops are crowded), shelves crammed with all manner of novelties from corncob pipes to plaster seagulls. Everything is here one remembers from the vacation visits to little shops (whose doors always stuck) jam-packed with treasures the likes of which never were seen elsewhere.

Sea Life is much larger than the shellporiums of memory. A large corner which extends shelves along each wall holds bins and boxes of agate, marble, slate, agatized wood, and thunder eggs, all sold by the pound; some polished, some "raw." Another wall is given over to bins and boxes of sea shells, from small pearly buttons the size of baby mushrooms to big horns that hum siren songs of the sea when held to the ear.

Rocky headlands and sea stacks rise abruptly from the pounding surf off Cape Meares, at Three Arch Rocks National Wildlife Refuge. Sea lions and migratory birds may be viewed from the beaches south of the cape.

A large collection of ship models shares a bank of shelves shoulder to shoulder with small mementos, hand-crafted or mass-produced mixed indiscriminately. Ceramic crab ashtrays, peanut shell figures seated on sand dollars, plaster pirates—what memories they evoke! One startlingly life-like caricature of a human face made from a short section of 2-inch pine limb, cut on the diagonal and painted with a plastic finish, fitted with plastic eyes, has a "mouth" which holds a toothbrush.

And there's more: driftwood mobiles, jewelry, glass and plastic floats hanging from a beam...and shell art. Remember the plaques with designs made from small shells glued on velvet backgrounds? Once inexpensive, current shell pieces often bear sizeable price tags. A $10'' \times 14''$ glass tray with a della Robbia border of piled shells here has an asking price of $24. Wall mirrors framed with shell borders sell for comparable prices.

There are still plenty of shell novelties available at small cost, however. And the most beautiful memento of the coast is still the least expensive—a single seashell exquisitely tinted in a rainbow-range of sea colors personally picked up on the beach.

Sea Life sits at the highway's edge in Rockaway.

The Whales

The whale, whose species have produced the most massive creatures ever to inhabit our planet, is having difficulty staying alive in a shrinking world. Technology which has, in effect, reduced the earth to a 24-hour circumference has also escalated threats to these peaceful mammals, as it has to all marine life.

Herds of blue whales—animals large enough for Jonah to have swum through their heart valves—have been reduced to an estimated 6 percent of their original population. Gray whales which once thrived in the world's oceans numbered only a few thousand by the 1930's. The Atlantic gray whales are no more. Only a group of California grays, protected by international treaty for the last 40 years, hold their own.

The semi-annual 8,000-mile journey by the grays from breeding grounds in Baja California to summer feeding grounds in the Bering Sea and back again—the longest migra-

A carved memorial panel (left) beside the parking area at the end of the South Jetty Road (Florence) commemorates the 41 sperm whales which beached themselves and died there June 16, 1979. Best time for whale watching on the Oregon coast is December through April in early morning. These mighty giants have roamed the world's oceans for over 50 million years. They are the deepest divers of any animal, communicate by voice over vast distances, and have the largest brains of any animal on earth. Carver George von der Linden contributed the carving on the marker placed by the Eugene Greenpeace Foundation.

tion of any animal—offers Oregonians a ringside seat to observe them often during the year.

The trip south begins in early fall and brings them close in to the Oregon shore. The most visible sign of their presence will be blow spouts—small feathery umbrellas of water against the sky—as they pass. If viewers are lucky, the whales may be seen breaching also, leaping from the water to silhouette briefly against the horizon in arcs which seem amazingly graceful, considering their bulk. Gray whales grow to lengths of 35-50 feet. The infants are 14-17 feet long and average 1,500 pounds at birth.

Sperm whales, deep-water feeders, are not so easily spotted during migration. When they do come in to shore, it is usually a matter of life and death, literally. Prime example is the beaching of 41 sperm whales near Florence the evening of June 16, 1979. By the time scientists and environmentalists reached the stranded whales, internal damage caused by their massive weight, minus suspension in water, made death inevitable.

A memorial marker in the parking area at the north end of the South Jetty Road in Florence commemorates this mass suicide of the creatures. Created by George von der Linden, the 6 foot-square carving of weathered cedar carries a simple statement describing the incident and the reminder that man shares the planet with other species, and all are depending on an interacting environment.

Best time for whale watching on the Oregon coast is December through April, in early morning. But they can be spotted any time from the headlands and viewpoints along the shore.

Cape Perpetua, the Oregon coast's highest promontory, which rises 800 feet above the ocean, offers excellent viewpoints for watching the gray whales as they make their annual 8,000-mile journey south each fall from the Bering Sea to Baja California. A side road leads to this viewpoint off U.S. 101 south of Waldport.

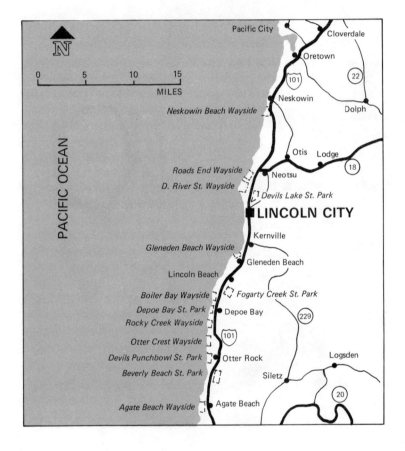

Lincoln City
Depoe Bay

LINCOLN CITY

Lincoln City is an amalgamation of small communities that includes Nelscott, Taft, Oceanlake, DeLake, and Cutler City which incorporated in 1965 to develop the area as a tourist center. The year-around population of 5,000 often swells to five times that number during the height of the summer vacation season. Lincoln City, at the top end of the Oregon coast's "Twenty Miracle Miles," offers every possible convenience and accommodation for travelers and vacationers, from campgrounds and RV parks to luxury motels that rank with the country's best; plus restaurants in a price scale that extends from the least expensive of the fast-food chains through to the finest of gourmet cuisine.

Recreational facilities abound. Along with natural beaches and lakes and streams—some of the loveliest in the world—are to be found superior shops, excellent golf courses, and superior galleries where the works of members of the growing fine arts community are displayed. Water sports are prominent among area activities.

To the south of the city is the **D River**, a narrow stretch of water 440 feet long that winds between shores strewn with driftwood from Devil's Lake on its short trip to the Pacific. Signs at north and south ends of the bridge across the little stream proclaim it the "world's shortest river." And so it is. In 1940 the US Geodetic-Geographic Board certified it as such, after determining its accurate length at low tide. And in 1973 the "Guiness Book of World Records" listed the D as the world's shortest, along with the Nile as the world's longest river.

Devil's Lake, the long curved body of water that feeds the tiny river, is Lincoln City's popular spot for water skiing and sailing, with trout fishing open year-round as well. But the real excitement comes in mid-September when boaters from all over the country join the annual hydroplane races. For two days, one-at-a-time racers skim across the water, often setting new world records. One enthusiast calls it "the Bonneville Salt Flats of sea racing." Indian legend has kept alive tales of a resident sea monster akin to Scotland's Loch Ness creature and British Columbia's Ogopogo who inhabits Lake Okanogan, but without their record of recorded sightings.

A public boat ramp, picnic tables, playground equipment, and restrooms are in Regatta Grounds Park on the lake. Similar facilities are found in the park area at the end of Holmes Road. Over 100 camping and trailer sites are available.

Kirtsis Park in the center of Lincoln City is home for a bronze statue of Abraham Lincoln, the work of Washington, D.C., sculptress Anne Hyatt Huntington. The statue was given to Lincoln City when the city was incorporated in 1965 by Governor Mark Hatfield, who felt it was the most fitting site for the statue presented as a give to the people of Oregon by the artist.

Interesting Activities

For 30 years **Lacey's Doll and Antique Museum** has been a landmark in the Lincoln City area. Originally from Salem, Oregon, Hazel Lacey and her son Dean have displayed their collection of over 4,000 dolls in the same location at 3400 Highway 101 for three decades and let the world come to them.

Dean Lacey estimates between 10,000 and 15,000 visitors a year view the cases of dolls in the long museum showroom. And they do indeed have tourists from around the globe.

Most of the dolls—some over 100 years old—are dressed by Mrs. Lacey; many of them wear authentic costumes. The dolls range in size from miniscule to life-sized (the latter a wax replica of Queen Elizabeth) plus a china doll 4 feet tall, and reproductions including such famous personages as Jenny Lind.

The Laceys are buying few new dolls these days. Doll collecting has grown to second place among collectors during the past 10 years, making suitable dolls for the museum costly and hard to find. But the present display can keep a doll buff busy for a long afternoon. Even the most casual viewers average an hour in the musuem, Lacey reports.

The Laceys also have a collection of antique china, and there are models of the pistols used to assassinate both Presidents Lincoln and McKinley in the antique gun collection.

But the drawing card here is the dolls—hundreds upon hundreds of them. The modest fee buys visitors the opportunity to browse through the past at their leisure.

In Lincoln City Plaza at the north end of town on Highway 101 you can find just about anything. The pivotal supermarket is supported by an assortment of variety shops.

Craft Junction—it's easy to lose an hour or so browsing this consortium of small stores in the plaza. Shop specialties here range from fine arts to candy to shoes to plants to woodcraft, with an ice cream parlor and a restaurant thrown in for good measure.

The Wine and Cheese Shop operated by Kip Ward and Sarah Robertson is chock full of quality cheeses, coffees, teas, jams—specialty eatables of all kinds. As for wines, it's safe to say you'll go a long way on the coast before you find the variety—ranging from the labels of Oregon wineries to quality imports—featured here. They carry over 650 wines, but don't expect to pick up a case of rare French vintage on impulse. Ward admits that many labels "in stock" are represented by a single bottle. "I just get a kick out of knowing that if someone comes in and asks if we have a Chateau Mouton-Rothschild I may be able to say 'Sure!'"

These friendly young people have tables covered with red-checked cloths in the back of the shop for customers who want to select some cheese and wine and enjoy it on the spot.

The **Bowsprit Bookshop** in Lincoln City is a book-browser's paradise. A relaxed atmosphere, induced by background music and places to sit while examining likely choices, reflects the owners' policy of going out of the way to please customers. The shelves are stocked with quality books in variety, attractively displayed. The people here are happy to special order without extra charge.

The Bowsprit is located in the Family Plaza on NW 15th Street and is open every day: Monday—Saturday 10 a.m. to 6 p.m.; Sundays, noon to 4 p.m.

Jane and Cullen Thielsen also operate the **Allegory Bookshop** (in the Marketplace across from Salishan Lodge at Gleneden Beach) which provides comparable pleasures for those who enjoy fine books.

Friendly Eating Places

Roads End Dory Cove—the restaurant with the dory on top (of a high pole)—is north of Lincoln City near Roads End Park. There traces of the road built by Phil Sheridan in the 1850's between coastal points and the Siletz Indian Agency 20 years before he became famous as a Civil War General can still be seen.

Seafoods are featured, steaks are available, but it is the clam chowder that is irresistible. It's a fun place to eat, and looks like a chowder house from a Disney production, with timbers hung with nets and floats among the plants, macrame window treatment, and tables centered with miniature yellow buoys which have menus printed on them. Prices at Dory Cove are on the reasonable side.

Pixie Kitchen, famed for its good food at affordable

prices, is straight out of Mother Goose. **Pixie Gardens** presents a three-dimensional view of fairyland guaranteed to delight children. This restaurant, listed as outstanding by such authorities as *Gourmet Times* and *Ford Times* magazine, goes all out to make this a pleasant stop for the whole family. Travelers will recognize this one a mile away.

Pier 101 restaurant and tavern, on the highway a couple of blocks south of the D River, is a comfortable place to enjoy a meal. Children are welcome in the restaurant.

The Cedar Tree at Salishan Lodge offers a superior specialty: potlatch salmon (barbecued on planks over charcoal) plus other seafoods, steaks. Summer season only, by reservation.

The Enchanted Dollhouse and **The Christmas Cottage** are too good to miss. For sheer enchantment you'll have a hard time surpassing an hour spent in this duo of small shops in the Nelscott Strip at 3259 SW Highway 101. Stepping through the door of the **Enchanted Dollhouse** is like stepping backward into childhood. The shop is crowded with dolls and accessories, most notably the elaborate dollhouses which are a specialty here. These lifelike houses of wood and shakes, beautifully crafted inside and out, are about as tall as a two-year-old, with large homey rooms upstairs and down. Some are assembled; some are sold as kits which are easily constructed into strong playhouses.

Four builders, some local and all in the state, work to keep up with the demand for these strong, creative dollhouses. And everywhere in the shop are furnishings for them. The expertly finished miniatures include everything from baby grand pianos to a full line of bathroom fixtures. Tiny lamps, pictures, rugs, and tableware are available.

Barbara Hasu, who with her husband operates the Enchanted Dollhouse, has the largest collection of miniature collectables on the coast. Limited editions of miniature ceramic plates, one *inch* in diameter, produced in lots of 250 by a Portland-area artist, signed and numbered especially for collectors are a specialty here. Both Christmas and Mother's

Day editions are sold out almost as soon as they are finished. A large mail order business includes repeat customers who add to their collections with each new run.

The Hasus also operate the **Christmas Cottage** next door, a year-round shop devoted exclusively to Christmas accessories—ornaments, gifts, wrappings, novelties. Christmas in July is more than a fanciful idea here. And, yes, you can find old-fashioned Christmas candle holders at Christmas Cottage; the kind that clamp on the branches with brackets for the small wax candles that were the forerunners of our twinkle lights. This is a fine place for people who like to get their Christmas shopping out of the way early.

Glassblowing has been transformed to fine art by the talents of Buzz Williams of **Alderhouse II**, Oregon's oldest glassblowing studio. He has refined the techniques of off-hand glass production and used it to create unique pieces in limited quantities as well as the more popular vases and containers.

Williams encourages visitors to watch as he teases the molten glass into works of art, designing as he goes. The basic ingredients of glass are lime, sand, and soda, but he doesn't have to start from scratch with his creations. He works with tons of recycled glass each year, using chemicals to add color and strength to the finished pieces. A 2,000-degree gas-fired furnace, used to heat the glass, must be kept fired around the clock, since it requires roughly two days to push the temperature back to the required intensity once it has cooled.

An hour spent watching the artisan working at this craft, which goes back to the Middle Ages, twirling and shaping the glowing blobs of near-liquid glass at the ends of his long hollow rod, evokes legends of alchemists. A mounting sense of excitement seems to transform observers into participants as an identifiable design emerges minute by minute. Truly, a glass-blowing studio is not "visited;" it is "experienced."

The geodesic dome which houses Alderhouse II is open to visitors from 10 a.m. to 5 p.m. every day, Mondays excepted, March through November. It can be found a half mile east of Highway 101 on Immonen Road (a pleasant shady drive) about ¾-mile south of the Siletz River bridge.

The Seagull Factory just behind Oceans West has its own spacious display—gulls perched on pilings under a ceiling hung with fish nets. Five craftspeople produce realistic seagulls made from concrete and painted with exterior acrylic paint, which weather for years. Some of them are usually at work putting finishing touches on these lifelike bird figures. They too are open every day throughout the year, except for Thanksgiving and Christmas.

Driftwood sculpture outside the Seagull Factory at Lincoln City is graced by one of the lifelike seagulls—made of cement and painted with exterior acrylic paint—which are manufactured there.

At **Oceans West Gallery**, 30 SE Highway 101, the work of 200 artists and craftspeople—most of them from the Northwest—is on display. Said to be the largest gallery on the coast, its spacious rooms make a wonderful place to browse and enjoy their fine selection of seascapes and other paintings. Wood chimes made of knives, forks, and spoons hung on stems of driftwood, functional pottery, and outstanding tole painting are among the varied items exhibited here. The gallery is open seven days a week, the year around.

Otter Crest

Otter Crest Loop—a four-mile stretch of low, curving coast road not integrated into Highway 101 where it climbs the heights between Depoe Bay and Newport—should be a priority side trip for visitors to the Oregon coast. The paved narrow road is draped along the lower cliffs like a strip of tinsel on a Christmas tree, providing intimate glimpses of pounding surf and secluded beaches from between thick coastal vegetation supplemented by panoramas of the primitive coastline from informal turnouts along the way.

The high point of the drive, literally, is the large State of Oregon observation area atop Cape Foulweather, named in 1778 by Captain James Cook. This first encounter with the Pacific Coast of North America by the British explorer was frustrated by an ocean storm of such magnitude it almost forced him to abandon his search for the legendary Northwest Passage; a search which took him finally to Nootka Harbor at Vancouver Island in late March.

The weather at the cape supports its name. At times fog swirls in so thickly it is like walking inside a cloud of damp smoke. The high chain link fence which protects visitors from deep chasms on two sides, the forested cliffs, are obscured within minutes.

But on a clear day you can, indeed, seem to see forever. Powerful telescopes allow close-ups of coastal birds and the white sea lions which play on the rocks offshore at low tide.

On the very edge of the 500-foot promontory beside the

parking area is **The Lookout Gift Shop and Observatory,** one of the best along the coast. Owners Kathryn and Ralph Peyton, for 17 years operators of Oregon's Crater Lake Resort, travel extensively to seek out unusual articles from around the world for the shop.

The Lookout gift shop on Cape Foulweather seems to hang like a crow's nest over the ocean, filled with unusual items from around the world. Stone figurines from Russia's Ural mountains, carved wooden bears from Hokkaido, marine figures fashioned by the Seri Indians of Baja California are just a few of the quality gifts to be found here. Shells in variety and quantity; marine brass; books by Northwest writers also find shelf space here. Telescopes mounted in the vista viewpoint area outside allow close-up looks at birds and sea lions on the rocks below. Cape Foulweather, named by Captain James Cook, whose ship was battered by a severe storm at this point, can be enveloped in a blanket of heavy fog without warning, its landmarks obscured within minutes. But on a clear day magnificent coastal views are visible for miles north and south.

The wide variety of quality gift items and art objects is evident as one steps into the shop, which seems to hang like a crow's nest over the ocean. Tiny figurines carved of semi-transparent stone from Russia's Ural Mountains shine with an inner luster highlighted by a finish treatment of hot paraffin. Wooden bears from Hokkaido, Japan's far-northern island, are made by the remnants of the primitive Ainu tribe, of whom there are fewer than 500 survivors.

Sharks, whales, and seals carved of ironwood from the Baja California desert by the Seri Indians are exquisite in their simplicity. The Seris, a stone-age tribe discovered only 60 years ago, have set up a production line for producing these flowing, satin smooth figures by hand. The members of the tribe—many of whom have never seen the animals they carve—block out the rough figures, which are then finished by the five master carvers of the tribe.

Shelves and cases are filled with special imported items: wood boxes decorated with enamel designs from Poland and woven water baskets from Africa compete for attention with jewelry from New Zealand shells of a radiant blue.

And that's only one part of the offerings to be found here. Bins and bins of seashells fill a small annex beneath collections of glass floats from one to 24 inches in diameter hanging from the ceiling timbers. These once-common beach finds are now collectors' items, traveling estimated distances up to 20,000 miles on ocean currents before being washed onto the coastal beaches.

The Lookout also features a marine museum which exhibits artifacts from wrecked ships which once carried supplies and goods for early traders and settlers in the Oregon country. A huge brass telescope estimated to be over a hundred years old has been in use at the shop since it was started in 1938.

A good selection of books by Northwest authors, or those about the Pacific Northwest Coast, offers a fine opportunity for browsing. Not to be overlooked either is an outstanding assortment of wildflower seeds, not easily found these days: beargrass, Indian paintbrush, harebell, wild hollyhock, dwarf lupine, and avalanche lily blend are among those offered from Spokane seedman Will McLaughlin's nursery.

The road continues on past the **Inn At Otter Crest**, one of the coast's superior resorts, whose timbered units cling to the hilly shoreline among the evergreens as if they too had dug roots into the rocky cliffs.

The drive, which begins at Whale Cove at the north end, rejoins the highway at the village of Otter Rock.

DEPOE BAY

A historical marker beside the bay describes the town's background. Indian Charlie Depot (so named for having worked at a United States Army Depot when Indians registered through the Siletz Agency were required to have English names for census rolls and recording of land holdings) was alloted lands around the Bay in 1894. The town was platted in 1927 and named DePoe—the family over the years having changed the spelling. When the post office was established the next year, the government further simplified the spelling at Depoe Bay, without the capital P.

Spouting horns along the rocky shore often send geysers shooting high into the air, on occasion squirting arches of water across the highway. But there is no predicting the timing of these natural displays, and visitors may be lucky enough to witness them any time of the year. Chances are best though in winter when ocean storms intensify breaker activity.

Things to See and Do

The flocks of seagulls using the jagged rocks at **Boiler Bay Wayside** as a launching pad for their wheeling flights over cascading waves seem unperturbed by the tides' assaults on the wild shoreline. Casual visitors often assume the name describes the ocean's frenzied activity here, until they discover the memorial sign which explains the bay is named for a boiler from a turn-of-the-century steam schooner, the *J.*

Marhoffer, which burned off Cape Foulweather May 19, 1910.

The wooden steamer was turned into an inferno within minutes when a gas torch, in the hands of an assistant engineer unfamiliar with its workings, ignited in the engine room. The *Marhoffer's* Captain Gustav Peterson ordered the helmsman to head the blazing vessel toward shore as the two lifeboats were launched. With 21 crew members, the captain and his wife watched as the flaming ship crashed into the shore rocks and exploded.

Interpreting as a warning the signals of a woman who ran to Fogarty Beach waving a red sweater to indicate a safe landing place, the survivors rowed two miles south to Whale Cove and landed safely. The ship's cook, badly burned, was the only casualty.

The rusty boiler eventually washed ashore at Boiler Bay. Now, burrowed into the sand, it is photographed by tourists, scoured by the tides, and is seemingly ignored by the gulls.

This is a pleasant stop for leg-stretching or lunch. There are 25 picnic tables and restrooms in the wayside, which offers spectacular scenic views of the ocean.

Depoe Bay is publicized as the world's smallest navigable harbor. But its six acres of water is headquarters for commercial and charter fishing fleets which rank among the finest on the Oregon coast. Completely equipped charter fishing boats offer deep sea trips, while excursions are available for sightseers.

The **Tradewinds Trollers** owned by Stan and Elsie Allyn is representative of the accommodations offered visitors who take advantage of the recreation offered through the Depoe Bay fleets. Deep sea charters begin at dawn and continue through the day, averaging four hours each, with longer trips offered by arrangement for groups of 6 or more.

Coffee and rain gear is provided, along with bait and tackle and fish bags. Icing and/or canning facilities are located in Depoe Bay for preserving the catch and making shipping arrangements also.

An angler's license for salmon (the only fish requiring one) can be obtained at the Tradewinds office on a daily basis.

On any sunny day—and often on stormy ones—the observation deck at the north end of the bridge at Depoe Bay is a favorite spot for vacationers watching the activity in the sheltered boat basin below. Charter boats depart and return to the docks below where fish caught by the clients of the deep-sea vessels are cleaned and packed in ice to be carried home.

Those who take the trip as non-fishing passengers may go for half fare.

Forty-minute excursion trips around the bay are also available through Tradewinds, with children under six riding free. The scenic cruise may include a close-up view of whales during their migrations up and down the coast.

For confirmed landlubbers, the thrill of the catch may be experienced vicariously by watching from the highway underpass viewpoints which overlook the docks as clients' catches are prepared for packing after each trip. The observation deck atop the Depoe Bay State Park building on the ocean side offers an excellent viewpoint for watching the Depoe Bay fleet boats enter and leave the harbor through the high rock walls of the narrow channel. Telescopes allow visitors to watch the boats far out from shore.

Harbor facilities here are easily accessible, and a wide variety of shops keeps visitors interested while waiting for cruises and fishing trips to begin.

Gift certificates are offered by Tradewinds and the other charter companies operating out of Depoe Bay: **Deep Sea Charters, Jimco Dock**, and **Pier I Sportfishing**.

An aquarium in a coastal town may seem redundant to the casual visitor. But travelers should not be misled into bypassing the **Depoe Bay Aquarium**. There are only two older aquariums in the United States. This one is truly, as its advertising proclaims, "like taking a walk on the floor of the sea."

The exhibits are presented in a background which simulates an undersea cave. Fish appear and disappear in rock-framed "windows" in an ever-changing show of grace and motion. The 1,600-gallon fish tank includes starfish and crabs, sea urchins, and anemones among its large assortment of ocean creatures.

Large specimens are on display also: a green sea turtle, for instance (they sometimes grow to over 800 pounds); a wolf eel (an adult can snap a 2×4 in its jaws); several octopi which can change color at will (deep red to white or vice versa) by manipulating the pigment cells of their skins.

But the main attraction is the small herd of harbor seals that live in the tiled pool in the grotto. These personable creatures are born entertainers who delight spectators by the tricks they perform when thrown pieces of fish, on sale in small packets for this purpose. It's worth the modest admission price for the seals alone; the rest of the exhibit is a bonus.

This is one of those special attractions which entrance children and adults with equal ease.

Shops and Marts in Depoe Bay

The Pacific Brass and Copper Works is just a tad off the highway but it's worth looking for. It's advertised as "the shiniest place on the Oregon coast" and you'd better believe it. Anything in brass and copper that the average traveler would find of interest can probably be found here, from nautical antiques to hardware. Visitors will have no trouble finding this shop next door to the old post office in Depoe Bay on the north side of the bridge. They're open four days a week—Wednesday through Sunday—10 a.m. to 6 p.m.

Pink Panther Gifts has handmade Indian jewelry; **Spindrift Gifts** features collector chess sets from all over the world, both north of the bridge on the highway.

The handcrafted door to **Foxythings Gifts** looks like an outsized gift package. Weathered boards placed on the diagonal form a background for wood cutouts of flowers and letters attractively mounted to identify the shop and establish the tone for the unusual stoneware pieces found inside. Pottery wine sets—carafes and glasses—of distinctive design and colors are especially noteworthy. But many of the pieces shown at **Foxythings** have unique touches which set them apart from the purely utilitarian pottery.

A charming group of buildings north of the seawall includes two attractive small galleries. **The Gaslight Gallery** specializes in fine arts, glassware, and pottery. **The American Gallery** runs more to gift items. Both are well worth browsing.

A Very Special Place

A visit to **Thundering Seas**, the school of jewelry design and manufacture, is a unique experience. Thundering Seas was developed to instruct students in age-old techniques of jewelry making and to train instructors in classical methods. Visitors bring an important emphasis to the operation.

The fine mineral museum is enough in itself to warrant a trip to the studio off South Point Road (a half mile south of the Depoe Bay Bridge) on Pacific Avenue. But more than that, visitors are welcomed into the workroom to watch students as they practice the fine art of creating in precious metals. It is possible for those coming to the studio to contract with students for custom jewelry designed to their specifications, which is not only less expensive than the same work executed by an established designer, but has the added benefit that both gems and metals used in jewelry produced at Thundering Seas is certified in writing.

Regular hours are from 10 a.m. to 4:30 p.m. five days a week (the studio is closed on Wednesday and Sunday) with other hours arranged by appointment.

Dining Out in Depoe Bay

The North Point Cafe, a small restaurant surrounded by window walls affords diners a wide-angle view directly into the bay. At low tide a recurrent pattern of shadows portrays a classic "Indian Brave" head in the shallow waters. Sea lions often frolic here to entertain patrons while their meals are being prepared. This is strictly a come-as-you-are eating spot, and it offers one of the loveliest views of the Depoe Bay waters.

The Sea Hag in the center of Depoe Bay is known up and down the coast for its food and entertainment. The newly decorated restaurant is inviting inside and out. They feature a Sunday Champagne Brunch, buffet specials during the week, and prime rib on Saturday nights; plus the Tufor Hour every day from 5-6:30 p.m.—two drinks for the price of one, and free hors d'oeuvres; with name performers and music for dancing from 8 p.m. A fun place any day in the week.

Tucked away in a bend of the hilly coast highway a couple of miles south of Depoe Bay is a delightful motel/ restaurant unit. **Whale Cove** is small, sitting among the trees on the edge of the cliffs overlooking a hidden inlet where the whales come in frequently to scrape the barnacles off against the steep rock walls on their way north. Rumor has it moonshiners once dumped a load of bourbon in the waters here to escape its being confiscated by government men.

Mike and Ann Crain are friendly, outgoing hosts who make patrons feel at home. And they offer good food to go with the good view seven days a week, with live entertainment Friday and Saturday evenings and Sunday afternoons.

Annual Events

The annual **Fleet of the Flowers** at Depoe Bay is held each Memorial Day. After special services, memorial wreaths are loaded onto boats which move slowly through the channel and out to sea where the flowers are tossed onto the ocean's surface as the boats parade in a circle around them to commemorate those from the area who have lost their lives at sea.

Each year in September a community **Indian Salmon Bake** is held at Fogarty State Park. Salmon baked on sticks thrust into the ground over fire trenches is served to the public at this yearly celebration of the salmon harvest.

Areas typical of the lush forest lands inhabited by the northern coastal Indians before the coming of white settlers can still be enjoyed in many of the state's parks. Oswald West State Park 10 miles south of Cannon Beach offers both ocean beaches and rain forest woods, plus 36 primitive camp sites.

The Indians

The Indians of the Oregon coast were different from their inland neighbors—lighter-skinned, finer-boned, who bathed often, cleaned their cedar-plank houses regularly and changed their beds by placing fresh evergreen boughs between new woven mats. They were boatmen instead of horsemen; harvesters instead of hunters.

Early explorers named them "flatheads," seeing most of the Salish and Chinook with flattened foreheads. Some bands shaped heads to a point in back; others forced them into a shelved ridge shape. But not all coast tribes practiced head shaping, and all had given it up by the late 1800's.

The salmon, food staple of the coastal Indians, was interwoven through their culture. As late as the 1940's a secret salmon festival was being held each year by Indians along the Columbia. Present-day Siletz Indians, seeking to recover from the federal government reservation lands surrounding the site of their former Indian Agency, have asked specifically to be awarded "a few hundred salmon a year for cultural purposes" in addition to the land.

Before wagon trails and railroads opened the coast valleys to public access, the Indian population was made up of bands, extensions of a dozen larger families. Languages spoken by these scattered bands were so diverse that when remnants of the groups were exiled to the reservation at Siletz in 1856, it was necessary for many of them to learn jargon—a mixture of Chinook, French, and English words which had become the *lingua franca* of the early Northwest—before they could understand each other.

Families varied in size from a few dozen persons to

several hundred. Thirty-six bands of the Chinook family lived along the south side of the Columbia; the Kusan family at Coos Bay had only three bands. The groups lived together without too much conflict. Their "wars" were often arranged by agreement between chiefs of the bands involved.

When Dr. John McLaughlin took over as governor of the Hudson Bay Company holdings at Fort Vancouver in 1825, he administered the profitable "fur preserve" and its inhabitants sternly but fairly for his time. But with the increasing immigration to the northwest during the next 15 years, stimulated by a depression in the United States, and spearheaded by the overland crossings of the missionaries, unrest began to grow among the Indians. The massacre at Wailatpu Mission near Walla Walla, in which missionary Doctor Marcus Whitman and his wife Narcissa were killed, set off a decade of conflict between settlers and natives of the Oregon Territory.

The grievances were heightened on both sides by the epidemic of gold fever which spread from California along the rivers of the Oregon border, and by the infiltration of settlers into the lush coastal lands, eager to stake claims there. The coast Indians were caught up in the resulting conflicts and in 1856 were literally herded onto reservations, either as a result of treaties (few of them honored) or as prisoners of war.

Some were taken to the reservation at Grande Ronde; most ended up at the Siletz reservation. Soldiers routed Indians from their homes, without warning in many cases, at the end of the Rogue wars, marching them to the new lands without provisions. With no household possessions, and the foreign names arbitrarily assigned to make record keeping easier for the agents, their traditional family groups were broken up.

From the beginning white settlers moved onto Indian lands almost as they chose, aided by government agencies which found means to remove the natives from their choice acres. The Siuslaws, who originally owned more than 500,000 acres along the Siuslaw River, were maneuvered into signing a treaty with the United States government in 1855 which specified payment in full of an agreed sum for their property. As late as 1970 payment had not been made.

With the formation of the Siletz reservation—a little over a million acres—many of the Siuslaws were transplanted there along with what was left of other family groups. But within 20 years these lands, too, had been placed in public domain and opened to homesteaders, except for areas close around the agency site. After the agency was closed in 1929, the Indians, many of whom homesteaded their own lands in the area, were gradually absorbed into the community. When the United States government formally terminated the Confederated Indian Tribes of the Siletz in 1954, the tribes no longer existed.

But in 1967 steps were begun to resurrect the Siletz tribal entity, and in 1977 they became the second tribe in the nation to achieve restoration. On September 3, 1980 the Siletz Indian Reservation Act was signed by President Carter, transferring 3,360 acres of federal lands, once part of the original Coast Reservation, to the tribe. In addition, the city of Siletz is restoring to them the 36-acre Agency site at Government Hill, which includes the Indian Cemetery transferred to the Tribal Association in 1975.

The restoration of status as a tribe was pushed partly to make the Siletz peoples eligible for education, medical and social benefits, and job training under government programs. But leaders emphasize that acquisition of the reservation will also help restore and preserve the cultural heritage which is fast being lost as individuals are absorbed into a white society.

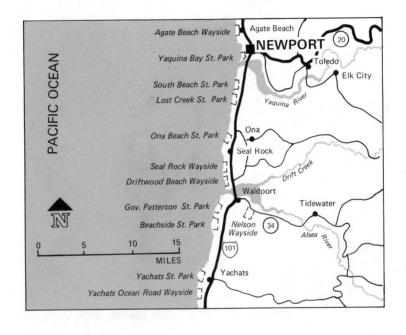

Newport
Waldport

NEWPORT

The Lincoln County Historical Museum next door to the Armory in Newport's center looks like one. The old log cabin shows the usual articles which chronicle a region's history: household goods, tools, machinery, and of course marine artifacts. Items in the fine Indian collection, mostly from those who came to be known as Siletz after being transplanted from many coastal areas to the Siletz Agency lands, were aquired from a former storekeeper who worked at the agency in the 1880's.

Historic Yaquina Bay Lighthouse in Yaquina Bay State Park was built in 1871. The county maintains the light station as a museum furnished in the style of the late 1880's, and visitor hours are observed on a regular schedule during the summer months.

The Marine Science Center encompasses many programs. To the quarter-million visitors who follow the curving road under the Yaquina Bay Bridge to the center's complex on the Bay each year, it appears to be a combination of museum and aquarium.

The exhibits section is open daily the year around for

"window views" of Oregon's marine life and close-up inspections of historical displays of diving suits, telescopes, and other nautical gear. And in the middle of the reception lobby is a touching pool where youngsters (oldsters too if they wish) are encouraged to get the feel of some of the sea creatures to be found along the coast. There's an opportunity for anyone so inclined to cozy up to an octopus, too, within limits.

The center has a bookstore which carries a fine assortment of printed materials relating to the Oregon coast, covering such subjects as polishing agates, collecting seashells, and of course a selection of seafood cookbooks.

The halls around the center courtyard often serve as hanging space for shows by Oregon artists and photographers which center around coastal themes. Vacationers can time their visits to the Seatauqua Summer Program sponsored each year by Oregon State University which presents a schedule of workshops, lectures, films, tours and other activities to involve and inform participants in coastal lore. Many of the activities, which take place from June through mid-September, are free. For workshops and tours a modest fee is charged.

Behind the scenes, so to speak, the Marine Science Center, under the guidance of Director Don Giles, has been the headquarters for OSU's research, teaching, and marine extension programs since it was built in 1965 in conjunction with the Port of Newport and the federal government.

In the main building research projects sponsored by both government and private agencies allow scientists to search for answers to problems of pollution, explore ways of utilizing the ocean's resources, and to study marine activity. Yaquina Head Station north of Newport serves the center as a site for beach-oriented programs and research projects.

The Center exhibits section is open daily 10 a.m.-4 p.m. (summer hours 10 a.m.-6 p.m.).

On the Waterfront

As with most coastal towns, Newport's waterfront seems to hum with a special energy. This is where most coastal settlements have their beginnings, and where their historic buildings are located usually; and often is where rejuvenation begins as old buildings which have survived the assaults of wind and storms imposed by accumulating years are remodeled to house new enterprises.

Newport's **Old Town** bayfront is a fascinating combination of past and future. Antique shops and modern galleries rub shoulders with tackle shops and charter boat offices. At **Neptune's Wharf** the two-masted sailing ship **Sara** is maintained in top-notch condition—a living monument to the days when sailing vessels afforded the main link between the Pacific Coast and the outside world. More than 500 sailing ships were built in Pacific Coast shipyards like those of the Simpson family at Coos Bay during the last half of the 19th century. The *Sara* is one of the handful that survive.

Visitors to the *Sara* can examine in detail the furnishings and fittings of the small ship, a masterpiece of efficiency in design which allowed ships' crew and officers (and often the Captain's family) to make long journeys halfway around the world in some semblance of comfort. Tour guides on duty during the summer will answer questions and explain the workings of the beautifully crafted ship.

Alongside the *Sara's* mooring is **Neptune's Village**, a gift shop which carries, in addition to the requisite gift items (pottery, sculpture, jewelry, and paintings), boutique wear, incense, mirrors, and other items, most of it handcrafted. It's a fun shop to browse for mementos and souvenirs. Their "littles" are special too.

Neptune's Wharf restaurant has been a landmark for a long time, where diners can enjoy fine seafood while watching the gulls and the boats on Yaquina Bay. Live music is featured weekends in the Dolphin Room.

The antithesis of Neptune's Wharf is *Mo's*, the little chowder house begun by a fisherman's wife to have hot food waiting at the wharf when the fishing boats came in. Mo's proudly boasts "We aren't fancy but we're famous!" And indeed they are. The fame of Mo's clam chowder has spread up and down the coast by word of mouth to the point where the original small cafe site has been supplemented by **Mo's Annex** across the street from the original cafe, plus a branch in an old cannery warehouse in Florence.

These are come-as-you-are places. Guests sit on benches at trestle tables wherever they can crowd in—because Mo's places are usually crowded, for good reason. Clam chowder is only the beginning of the good stuff they serve up. Louis-type salads are piled high with shrimp or crab; the slumgullion is something to rave about, and they make a blackberry cobbler better than anything mother used to bake.

There's one more place along the bay which shouldn't be missed. **The Whale's Tale** not only serves up some delicious food; the unusual decor is a visual delight to match. Their specialty is poppy seed pancakes served with honey, but their omelets aren't to be sneezed at, either. (Example: the Fisherman—fresh vegetables and cheeses topped with oysters sauteed in butter). Breakfast is served 7-11 a.m. weekdays, until noon on Saturdays and 1 p.m. on Sundays. They stay open until 10 p.m. on weekends, until 9 p.m. on weekdays, and are closed on Wednesdays.

On around Bay Boulevard, where it merges with Moore Drive, is **The Embarcadero**, Newport's fine resort/marina. **The Embarcadero** offers condominium-style accommodations: one- and two-bedroom apartments with fireplace and kitchen, plus studio units, at prices that are well in line with local motels. The problem may lie in obtaining reservations.

The Embarcadero's excellent moorage facilities can handle any craft from outboards to cruisers. Beautifully situated for vacation fishing (your boat or theirs from their rental fleet), the marina is popular with those wishing to relax and fish with the least hassle possible. Rental service includes all needed gear for clamming and crabbing, as well as for fishing.

Recreation facilities include play areas for children, a swimming pool, sauna, and whirlbath. Outdoor fishing piers are complete with cleaning stations, plus barbecues and crab cookers for outdoor parties.

It's just minutes away from beaches and coastal attrac-

Visitors are silhouetted against the Yaquina Bay Bridge as they leave Neptune's Wharf, framed by the rigging of the historic sailing ship **Sara**, now a museum on Newport's waterfront. The **Sara**, built in Oregon shipyards during the heyday of the sailing ships, is now open to the public.

tions, offering every convenience for the family vacation (except housing pets) or convention gatherings.

The Floating Aquarium

The Underseas Gardens on the bay in Newport is, literally, a floating aquarium; one big half-million gallon tank wrapped around the viewing room. The more than 5,000 exhibits—most from the coastal waters around Newport—have attracted four million visitors to date.

Marine life exhibited in a natural environment is reason enough to draw visitors by the thousands, but there are also special added attractions that make this more than your run-of-the-mill aquarium. "The World's Only Underwater Theatre" presents an underwater act complete with scuba divers and Aquamaids, plus a narrator to describe the marine animals pointed out by the diver. This hourly show stars Armstrong the Giant Octopus in a truly unique performance.

The Gardens are open daily 10 a.m.-5 p.m. (until 9 p.m. in summer) major holidays excepted. Young and old will find this "garden at the bottom of the sea" a delightful way to spend an hour.

Charter boats line up at their docks in Yaquina Bay like toys at the edge of a pond. Their bright colors and delicate appearances are deceiving, however; these are the vessels which carry eager fishermen out across the harbor bar to fish deep waters in the hope of experiencing the excitement of pulling in a big one.

Newport Sportfishing, operated by Ralph and Pat Wonsyld, is the largest of the charters headquartered on Yaquina Bay. The names of their boats evoke visions of those faraway islands in the South Seas. *Taku* and *Chiloquin* each carry 20 passengers; *Kai-Aku* can handle 17. The six-passenger boats have less exotic names: *Nana Ruth*, *Cod Father*, *Pastime II*, and *Bimini*.

Newport Sportfishing is based at the Embarcadero, and they offer every service the most particular devotee of charter fishing could ask for, from 24-hour phone service for reservations to payment by credit card. Fishing trips can be arranged for four, five, six, or eight-hour stints, for private parties or groups. Clients will have all bait and tackle furnished when they board the electronically-equipped craft. Free coffee is standard.

No license is required for bottom fishing. All charter offices on the bay can supply salmon licenses, either annual or on a daily basis.

Smaller charters on Yaquina Bay include the **Deep 6 Marina** (6-16 passenger boats); **Rich's Tradewinds** (6-10 passengers); **Seagull Charters** (6-10 passengers).

During the summer **Jet Boat Trips** makes 12 excursions daily between 9 a.m. and 6 p.m. from Neptune's Mooring.

Experienced pilots licensed by the Coast Guard guide the hydro-jets on the 10-mile trip around the bay and up the Yaquina River at half-hour intervals. Visa and Mastercharge cards are accepted, and fares reasonable. Group trips may be arranged in advance.

Whether fishing or excursioning, a boat trip allows passengers to see Yaquina Harbor and Newport from a new perspective.

And Up on the Hill—

A block or so up the hillside from the waterfront is **Canyon Way Bookstore**. Inside the rustic building are books by the carloads on just about any subject you care to pursue. The open building with its rough beam construction is a "nooks and crannies" place for sure: the children's books tucked into one section, specialty books in others. It's the kind of shop visitors can't help browsing in. Exploring one corner just naturally leads to another. An hour flies by in this inviting bookstore operated by Roguey and Edward Doyle. Open 10 a.m.—5 p.m. every day except Sunday.

The **Centre Restaurant** in the same building is open for lunch and dinner. The food is something special indeed: quiche and crepes and specialty sandwiches on homemade bread; soups. All this and cheesecake too!

The Royal Pacific Wax Museum

A wax museum is a wax museum, right? You see one, you've seen them all. Perhaps that truism explains the fascination of these displays of life-like figures which draw visitors by the thousands year after year. It's like taking a walk through a familiar picture album.

The figures at the **Royal Pacific Wax Museum** in Newport are from the studios of the famous Josephine Tussaud in London, England. Constructed and lavishly costumed there, these replicas of famous people afford a unique glimpse into history.

The world's famous and infamous are depicted here: leaders such as Stalin and Churchill; Presidents John Kennedy, Franklin Roosevelt, Washington, and Lincoln. Kings, queens, literary figures, and authors are to be seen also, the "goats" separated from the "sheep" in the Chamber of Horrors.

And for the children, an Enchanted Forest presents their favorite storybook characters in scenes from familiar fairy tales.

There's a gift shop, too. But the big attraction is a close-up view of famous people more familiar to most of us than our not-too-distant ancestors. Visitors are welcome to take pictures. They're open every day in downtown Newport. The white stucco building with the flags on top is easy to spot as you drive through town.

Sea Towne is a cluster of gray buildings, joined together to form a covered modern shopping mall just north of Newport. Among the shops found in the complex is **Land's End Gifts**, where you can find nautical brass and artifacts, metal sculptures, paintings, and other hand-crafted items.

Latte's Pacific Sea-Pak is a specialty products store which features Oregon labels with, naturally, an emphasis on seafood: smoked crab legs, tuna, oysters, and such. They carry gift packs of these fine products as well and will mail them anywhere in the world.

Before leaving Sea Towne, check **Merlowe's Coffee Bin** for special coffees and teas and the things that go with them.

A coast town without candy shops doesn't quite make it. Newport has no worries in that department. A long-time favorite, **West Homemade Candies** has products that are beautiful to the eye as well as to the tongue, and they too will mail anywhere. They're located on Highway 101 about half-way through town.

Down on the bayfront **Aunt Belinda's Salt Water Taffy** shop offers almost three dozen flavors, including butter-scotch, plus a big bunch of other goodies from all over the world.

At the south end of town near the approaches to the bridge is **Bridge Bakery**. The cases in this small, plain establishment are filled with baked goods of all kinds that taste as delicious as they smell. For those who can't wait to get home with their loot before sampling it, there are paper-covered tables and a coffee station where, for the price of a cup of coffee, you can sit down and enjoy your purchase. The friendly people who wait on visitors will even furnish a knife to those who lacked the foresight to buy doughnuts or danish instead of a big luscious pudding cake.

Agate Beach Artistry welcomes visitors every day. This fine-arts gallery/gift shop is a wonderful place to browse and buy: prints by Oregon artists, scrimshaw in an assortment of jewelry pieces (they'll take custom orders); plus crystal, glass, weaving, and pottery; imported jewelry and a toy section; shells and hand-crafted items too.

The **Potworks**, established four years ago in Waldport by Potter Jim Gore and relocated now in Newport, is the showcase for the quality stoneware which is his trademark. His pieces have style and are appreciated not only by travelers and vacationers in the area but by regional clients as well. Jim created and executed the tableware for the Iron Kettle dinner house in Waldport and the lamps in the Waldport Bakery.

Visitors to the Potworks are welcome to browse and watch Jim work at his new site in Old Town.

Uptown Eateries

House of Almerik—Steak and seafood (scampi, lobster, crab sauteed in butter and wine) plus garden salad, sourdough bread, and extras. By reservation, in South Beach, 121 Pacific Highway South.

The Towne House—three miles north of Newport on Highway 101. A quality dinner house specializing in seafood with something extra: bouillabaise, crab legs, Pacific oysters; a special children's menu. Prices reflect the quality of the food, on the up side, but worth it. And thrown in for free—a "million dollar view of the ocean" while you dine in style.

4 J's Restaurant, 614 Elizabeth, is Newport's only ocean-front eating house. The prices are reasonable; the food is good, especially their breakfasts.

Swedish Smorgasbord for those who like to help

themselves: a wide assortment of salads and desserts to supplement everyday standbys—meat balls, deep fried ling cod,
stroganoff—plus daily meat specials and homemade Swedish
bread. It's just north of the bridge on the highway.

Annual Events

Loyalty Days is a traditional celebration which has been
observed in Newport the weekend nearest May 1 for over 20
years. The first observation of Loyalty Days was organized
by Veterans of Foreign Wars as a response to counteract the
annual May Day celebrations by Communists. From that
first parade composed of area veterans, the festivity has
grown to include a parade made up of scores of entries, plus
military units and a queen's court, and of course veterans.

A fluctuating program of activities keeps things moving
during the four days of festivities, changing from year to year
to include such activities as watershows, dances, crab feeds,
cycle races, square dances, art shows, talent shows; plus the
Sailing Regatta now held in conjunction with the Loyalty
Day celebration.

There's always a Coast Guard ship on hand, too, where
visitors may come aboard, with Coast Guard personnel to
conduct guided tours.

The Loyalty Day Bill was signed into law by President
Eisenhower in 1957, but Newport had already tucked two
celebrations under its belt by that time. Loyalty Day is now
being celebrated in other communities around the state, but
Newport led the way.

The Seafood and Wine Festival is held the weekend nearest Washington's birthday, sponsored by the Newport
Chamber of Commerce. It features Oregon wines and local
seafood specialties.

The Blessing of the Fleet, sponsored by the Fishermen's
Wives Association, is held in early March in memory of
persons lost at sea.

Sea Gulch can be labeled a tourist attraction without
reservation. There's no way travelers along Highway 101
can miss it where it sits on a rise like some forgotten relic of

Western characters hand-carved with a chain saw crowd the front yard of the Sea Gulch to create a "wild and wooly west" tourist attraction. Billed as the largest collection of chain saw art in the world, demonstrations of the craft are held at intervals during each day. Six acres of "The Out Back" offer tableaus of chain-saw figures in natural settings, including a family of Bigfoot creatures.

the Old West, surrounded by a yardful of near-lifesize carvings. Ray Kowalski, its originator, proclaims it the fastest growing tourist attraction along the Oregon Coast.

The **Outback**—six acres of forest land people with carved wood figures created entirely by chain saws—is worth exploring if for no other reason than to snap photographs of a "family of Bigfoot," the Pacific Northwest's equivalent of Sasquatch and the Abominable Snowman.

Stock characters of the western frontier are all over the place, including a Boot Hill exhibit. Frequent demonstrations of chain-saw carving show onlookers how the exhibits are produced.

A gift store—**The Dry Gulch**—specializes in silver and turquoise Indian jewelry, and ivory scrimshaw. Other shops in the complex are **Seal Rock Woodworks** (wall carvings, furniture, and signs); **Gull's Hideaway** (driftwood art, handcrafted gifts); **Jolie's** (custom T-shirts).

They're open the year around, seven days a week.

SEAL ROCK

Seal Rock is the terminal of the Corvallis/Yaquina Bay wagon road, the first one to link the coast with the interior valleys of the state.

Hidden behind the picnic area of **Seal Rock Wayside** three miles north of Waldport is one of Oregon's most delightful beaches. Protected to the north by titanic cliffs and monoliths, the small beach manages to retain an air of seclusion. There's usually someone fishing from the rocks in the shallows, silhouetted against sea and sky. The clamming is excellent here. Artists sometime perch on convenient overhangs trying to capture in sketches the restless beauty of waves crashing against rocks and invading the chasms among the roots of the rock cliffs. Hikers can't resist the narrowing bridge of cliff sand which scoots up to the top of the highest rocks. And photographers can't resist the chance to photograph these adventurers outlined against the sky.

Like many others along the Oregon coast, the beach at Seal rock Wayside offers sheltered places to build a fire for roasting wieners and toasting marshmallows or just for keeping warm when the wind blows.

WALDPORT

Waldport, situated in an area once encompassed by the Siletz Indian Reservation, was opened to white settlers in 1875, who promptly panned $1,700 in gold dust from the beach sands nearby.

In 1881 the post office was established, and three years later the town was platted, the streets laid out by the stars. Today Waldport is developing into a retirement town. The moderate weather, leisurely pace, fine fishing, plus excellent community facilities make this an ideal location for retirees.

The population remains under 1,000, although that could

change as more and more people find their way to the restful little coast town where there's always "plenty of nothing" to do, and plenty of time to get it done without hurrying.

Trident Antiques, Waldport, operated by Maren and Mike Taylor for the past nine years, is one of the largest on the Oregon Coast. A prolific stock ranges from carved pianos through marble-topped pieces, plus glass and china, to accessories which include a child's rocking horse made of a tiny carousel pony, bare of paint. Trident is fun for casual browsers, rewarding for collectors. Their **Reproduction Room** next door holds replicas of antiques at affordable prices. Outstanding items include bowl-and-pitcher stands topped by adjustable mirrors. Especially attractive are those fitted with soft blue enamelware decorated with deep pink flowers. Toys here are charming. An iron horse-drawn beverage wagon is complete with miniature wooden cases holding tiny Coca-Cola bottles. Trident is open seven days a week the year around, except Christmas and Thanksgiving.

Recommendable Restaurants

The Iron Kettle, the family restaurant and lounge on Highway 101 in Waldport.

The Experience, three miles east of Waldport on the Siletz Road; the fine eating place where they do original things with seafood. Reservations suggested.

Homes Away From Home

Scattered along the Oregon coast are the cottage motels, survivors from a simpler era of vacationing, now upstaged by the glass and stone and rustic-beam resorts developed to provide deluxe accommodations for an increasingly affluent society.

Waldport has several of these older motels tucked away in sheltered spots or snugged down at some choice beach location. They're small—a dozen or less units—and they go back to the days when a vacation at the coast meant finding a home away from home for a week at the beach. They have an air of belonging wherever they happen to be, and indeed for long-time vacationers in the area they now serve as landmarks. Most are equipped with kitchens, and many have fireplaces, because one of the joys of those earlier vacations was the good feeling of settling down with a bowl of popcorn in front of an open fire after a day on the beaches, safe from the pounding seas and the wind rattling at the windows.

For families who want to stay for any length of time, the favorable rates, compared to those of the larger and newer places, are attractive budget stretchers.

Some comfortable "littles" in the Waldport area:

Cape Cod Cottages—an oceanfront motel with fireplaces, kitchens, and TV.

Edgewater Motel—fireplaces, kitchens, sun decks, TV; units to accommodate parties from two to eight persons.

Sundown Motel—beachfront with ocean view; kitchens, TV, winter rates.

Sea Stone Cottages—kitchens, some fireplaces, TV; weekly and monthly rates, or overnight.

Terry-a-While-Motel—most with kitchens; multiple bedrooms for larger parties.

All of these are on Highway 101 within two to five miles of Waldport, on the south side.

The graceful waves and trenches of the 50-mile stretch of dunes which make up Oregon's "Sahara by the Sea" seem to echo the motion of the cresting ocean waves. From 2½ to 4 miles wide, the dunes advance inland up to six feet a year. Shaped by the wind in ever-changing patterns, this dune area contains some of the world's highest sand formations. Fresh-water lakes which are scattered through the sand hills were created by the advancing dunes damming up small streams. Areas of the Oregon dunes are open for camping and exploration.

The Dunes

Oregon recreationists have one of the world's largest sand piles at their doorstep: 32,000 acres of majestic dunes stretching almost 50 miles along the coast between Florence and Coos Bay. Since 1972 this enormous area of sand hills—two and a half to four miles wide—has been incorporated into the Oregon Dunes National Recreation Area designated for public enjoyment.

This active coastal area, ever-changing as the sea, advances north and east at approximately 6 feet a year. Sections have been stabilized by plantings of beach grass, shore pine, and the beautiful Scotch broom which, in season, splashes the coast landscape with sun-yellow blossoms where highways, channels, and other permanent installations must be protected from the encroaching areas.

The growth process of the dunes is a continuing cycle. The underlying sandstone base of the Oregon Coast Range mountains, perpetually eroded by the coastal climate, is whirled off to the ocean during spring flooding, only to drift back to land on westerly currents. The sand formations parallel the tidal action of the ocean, lapping in waves across the shore and building to spectacular heights. The world's largest sand dune rises to 380 feet in the Woahink Lake area near Florence.

The dunes are sprinkled with clear, sparkling, fresh-water lakes, as if a giant had tossed a handful of emeralds and aquamarines at random across its surface. Along the eastern edge of the recreation area the famous "fishing lakes" sprawl. Most of them bear Indian names: Woahink (Clear Lake), Tahkenitch (Lake of Many Arms), Cleawox (Lake in the Dunes) among them. Woahink Lake is indeed a clear deep blue; fed by fresh-water springs, it serves as the water supply for residences around its edges. To the west of the highway is Lake Cleawox, site of Lane County's Girl Scout Camp, divided by the ONDRA boundary; and one of the "many arms" of Tahkenitch Lake reaches inside the line.

Clear Lake, south of Reedsport, borders the highway. This is the only fenced lake in the group, and recreational use here is prohibited. A short distance farther, Eel Lake curls in a tight sickle shape, with the twin Tenmile Lakes fitting around and below it.

The lakes, large and small, were formed by sand dunes blocking the channels of streams in their relentless march inland. Over the centuries they have also smothered a giant evergreen forest, except for small islands of trees which show here and there among the ridges.

The dunes, like the sea, appear deceptively benign. People using the area are cautioned about some of the hazards which are ever-present, especially for children. Bulletins and signs remind vacationers that the sand near popular regions can contain broken glass and other debris which is buried by the shifting landscape; that it is easy to become lost in the dunes where wind action can wipe out footprints in an instant, and fog often creeps in swiftly; that dense undergrowth can cause panic, especially near dusk; that dry tips of beach grass can cut like razors; and that areas at the base of high mounds can be dangerous if dune buggies are in the vicinity.

Specific areas of the dunes are closed to vehicle traffic. One near Florence and another in northern Coos County prohibit vehicles from May through September; others are reserved for pedestrians the year around, including 3,000 acres of the highest dunes located in the Umpqua Scenic Area below Winchester Bay.

Campers are also cautioned about care with campfires. Dunes vegetation is full of oil and a fire, once started, can spread over large sections within minutes.

The dunes area is bracketed by Horsfall Beach, one of the longest on the coast, near Coos Bay; and by Honeyman State

Park, one of the area's loveliest, to the north at Florence. Honeyman has tent, trailer, and improved camping sites in abundance, plus all recreational facilities which include over 100 picnic sites in the beautifully maintained park.

The dunes area is under the jurisdiction of the United States Forest Service, with headquarters at 855 Highway Avenue, Reedsport, OR 97467.

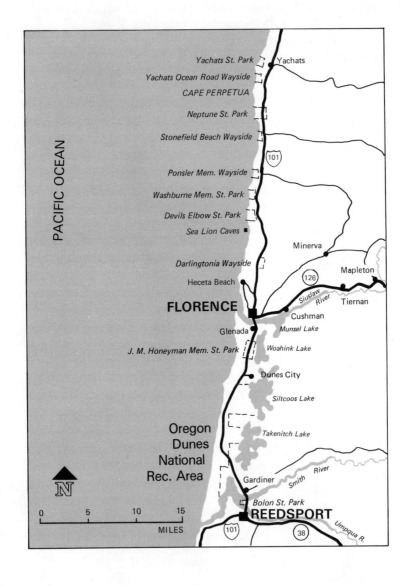

Yachats St. Park   Yachats

Yachats Ocean Road Wayside

CAPE PERPETUA

Neptune St. Park

Stonefield Beach Wayside

101

Ponsler Mem. Wayside

Washburne Mem. St. Park

Devils Elbow St. Park

Sea Lion Caves

PACIFIC OCEAN

Minerva

Mapleton

Darlingtonia Wayside

126

Heceta Beach   Tiernan

FLORENCE

Siuslaw River

Cushman

Glenada   Munsel Lake

J. M. Honeyman Mem. St. Park   Woahink Lake

Dunes City

Siltcoos Lake

Oregon
Dunes
National
Rec. Area

Takenitch Lake

Smith River

Gardiner

N

Bolon St. Park

0   5   10   15   REEDSPORT

Umpqua R.

MILES   101   38

Yachats
Florence
Reedsport

YACHATS

Yachats (pronounced Yah-hots) is a jewel of a vacation village snuggled up at the base of the coastal hills on the north shore of a small promontory which brackets the mouth of its namesake river. The tiny town of 500 people reflects a pleasing blend of resort/retirement community. While tourism is a vital element in its survival, there is little of the obviously commercial development in evidence.

The pleasures offered vacationers here are those provided by sandy beaches, small coves, convenient fishing sites, quality shops, and excellent restaurants and motels, all somewhat understated. Yachats is one of the places on the coast where vacationers come to "get away from it all" rather than to "be where the action is." People retire here for the same reasons. It is quality, not quantity, that is offered here.

The headquarters of the Coast Range Indian Reservation was located here during the mid 1800's, and the area contains shell mounds which accumulated over hundreds of years at the ceremonial meeting places of the coast Indian bands. Unfortunately they are disappearing as more and more people discover the serendipities of retiring near the sea.

Interesting Places

The Devil's Churn Wayside three miles south of Yachats is a deep chasm in the shoreline where the tides thunder and crash against the rocky walls to froth like whipping cream. Walkways and railed paths lead down to observation points close to the churning activity through shady forest groves, with panoramic views of the coastline from the high points.

The **Cape Perpetua Visitor Center** dispenses information which will help visitors understand and appreciate the Oregon coast: geologically, historically, and esthetically. It is a focal point to coordinate the wonders of nature which surround this area of the coast in ways that will allow travelers and vacationers to enjoy these natural phenomena on their own.

In the 47-seat auditorium at the center, a short motion picture entitled "Forces of Nature" details the drama of the rocky headlands and sandy coves shaped by the relentless assaults of wind and water against the shore, and of the creatures which inhabit this area. Dioramas highlight the history of human beings and their effect upon the area.

A receptionist on duty at the information desk will answer questions and suggest points of interest to be enjoyed. A promenade deck offers a panoramic view; restrooms and drinking fountains are here too.

Trails with poetic names lead out from the center. **The Trail of the Restless Waters** goes to the Devil's Churn; the **Trail of the Whispering Spruce** takes visitors 800 feet above sea level; **Saint Perpetua Trail** goes to the highest point of the cape. And there are others—

A self-guided auto tour turns off from the road above the visitor center that leads to the top of the cape, twisting and turning and climbing along a narrow paved route (most surely a revamped logging road) through lovely forest areas to the top of the ridge littered with felled skeletons of trees. Forest Service signs which blend with the natural background indicate special areas of trees and flowers.

The road roller-coasts for 22 miles through forested hills

A stroll on the beach at the ocean's edge as late afternoon shadows lengthen and early evening mists begin to roll in is one of the most pleasurable activities for coast visitors; a soothing alternative to the hustle-bustle of today's busy life.

before rejoining the highway at Yachats. This is truly a breathtaking ride, and for those uncourageous souls who retreat in the early stages, the downhill retracing offers some spectacular glimpses of blue sea far below, framed by forest giants that seem to stretch hundreds of feet before touching paler sky.

The visitor center is located in the Siuslaw National forest of 620,000 acres, one of the few national forests which includes a seacoast. An entrance a fourth of a mile north is the start of the auto tour and cape loop drive, and also leads to the Cape Perpetua Campground with facilities for both picnicking and overnight camping.

The cape, highest point on the Oregon coast, was named by English explorer Captain James Cook March 7, 1778, for Saint Perpetua who was martyred in Carthage March 7, 203 AD, for professing her belief in Christianity.

The center is open 8 a.m. to 6 p.m. May through September; in winter months, visiting hours are 10 a.m. to 4 p.m. Wednesday through Sunday.

The Muriel O. Ponsler Wayside is a small park fenced by a low stone wall which bears the marks of the masonry work provided by the Civilian Conservation Corps, the "army" of young men who enlisted in the CCC during the Depression of the 1930's. The land was donated to the state by Jack Ponsler for "public use and enjoyment" as a memorial to his wife. A few picnic tables, rather secluded, offer serene vistas of the ocean. An ornamental drinking fountain centers the park area, and through the years old-fashioned violets, wild strawberries, and daisies have spread to form a carpet of wildflowers in the spring. This is a delightful spot for lunching.

A couple of miles down the road toward Florence, **Carl G. Washburne State Park**, both sides of the highway, has some of the most inviting trailer sites among the coast's many lovely state parks. Low coast pines form green walls around spaces to give them a wonderful feeling of privacy. Winding forest roads through the park add to this sense of remoteness although neighbors may be right next door. A community kitchen and bathhouse are on the west side of the highway. Trails from the east side sector lead through the woods to the beach. The campgrounds offer 58 trailer spaces with utility hookups, two tent sites and nine picnic locales.

The Prehistoric Life Museum—FREE ADMISSION. That's what it says and that's what it means. But apparently the old truism that "No one values what isn't paid for" holds true here. This is the one a lot of people save for the "next trip."

They're making a mistake!

The museum between Yachats and Florence is a delight for anyone with an interest in fossils and/or rocks. Owner David Douglass refers to prehistoric ages as others reminisce about early childhood. Perhaps to a man surrounded by hard evidence of survival millions of years old, past and future are truly one.

The exhibit includes fossils of a dinosaur egg, a dragonfly, the usual bones and teeth and shells of animals who existed eons ago, and of course, fish. It is cased and detailed and illustrated by pictures.

Douglass' **Down to Earth Rock Shop** features agates and other native stones, thundereggs, and petrified wood. But he has extras too; equipment of all kinds, including cutting materials, and even gold pans. Literature on rock hunting and related activities is also found here. Customers for the rocks are collectors, rockhounds, and jewelers. But his most enthusiastic audience in the museum are children who are fascinated by the extinct creatures who roamed the continent milleniums ago.

May 15 through September the museum is open and waiting for visitors. The rest of the year visitors take their chances on finding anyone home. But it's worth a try.

Shops and Such

Products of Ken and Herta Koogler, operators of **Oregon Myrtlewood** just north of Yachats are displayed in a pleasant showroom which fronts the factory. The former cabinetmaker turns out an assortment of wood tableware and home accessories, assisted by his wife, who does spraying and band saw work. Most of it is finished in the softer tones that have replaced the high-lacquer finishes on much of the myrtlewood manufactured in earlier years. Myrtlewood requires special care in curing, so that a period of several years must elapse between harvesting and manufacturing. But the results are worth the waiting, as evidenced here by the gift wares shown. **Oregon Myrtlewood** is open the year around, except for Tuesdays during the "worst of the winter."

The Sea Fair Gift Shop in the small white buildings across from Beulah's in Yachats displays an outstanding selection of gift items produced by Oregon artists and craftspeople. Dee Cavanaugh, a former legal secretary from Portland, has made a point of stocking The Sea Fair with the works of regional artisans. The emphasis is on superior quality. The results of her efforts are apparent.

The smooth-flowing marine sculptures carved from coastal woods by Ray Chin compete for attention with his exquisite ink drawings; clocks made of driftwood by 74-years-skilled Asall Jepperson; hand-print notes by Betty Stockman; and photography by Ron Anicker are just a few of the fine gift items sold here.

Those who stop by can also see the dollhouse Dee is furnishing and decorating which stands in a corner behind the counter.

Of Ships & Sea is a museum/salesroom offering a superb selection of nautical antiques and reproductions in the tidy blue building which appears too small to hold such a variety of items. Displays include brass and copper (from lanterns and diving helmets to bells and chart weights) plus marine flags, figureheads, whistles, and small hand-crafted sea chests.

The shop, on Highway 101, three miles south of Cape Perpetua, sits on a cliff at the sea's edge, formerly the site of huge Indian shell mounds. Of Ships and Sea is open the year around, seven days a week.

Beulah's Sea View Inn has been a landmark in Yachats for so long it's hard to remember the time when the restaurant was not there. Originally housed in one of the small buildings propped up beside the highway where it curves around coming into town from the south, Beulah's has evolved into one of the fine dinner houses on the coast. The specialty here is chicken and dumplings, but in truth anything served at Beulah's is special.

The restaurant at **The Adobe** motel serves food which compliments the million-dollar view of the ocean from the dining room.

The **Yachats Pie and Kite Shop** is that "something special" place for lunches and breaks no one should miss! The little shop tucked away on Ocean View Drive a block or so west of Buelah's really does combine pies (home baked by the proprietors) and kites (from around the world). They open at 11:30 a.m.; they're closed Tuesdays. Customers know the pies are out of the oven when they see a kite flying from the building.

Annual Events

Yachats by the sea is one of the few places in the world where sea-run smelt come in to shore. From May through September the mating silver smelt come onto the beach by the thousands to be netted by local fishermen in specially designed smelt nets.

Each year in early July Yachats celebrates the smelt run with a **Community Smelt Fry**. Visitors from all over the West come in numbers which almost rival the smelt catch for this yearly feast.

In **Smelt Beach Park Wayside** overlooking the sandy beach where netters gather each year to harvest the small fish, a metal sculpture silhouetted against the sea makes a natural frame for offshore fishing boats for vacationers with cameras.

An annual **Arts and Crafts Fair** in March offers an opportunity for visitors to view the works of many fine regional artists and artisans who live along the Oregon coast.

Smelt Beach Park Wayside at Yachats borders the length of beach where netters come by the thousands each year to harvest the silver smelt with specially designed nets. This region is one of a few places in the world where the small fish come to mate. A community smelt fry—held annually to celebrate the smelt run—draws visitors from all over the West Coast.

FLORENCE

Florence, the town named after a board floated in from a shipwreck bearing that name, is the halfway point on the Oregon coast. The settlement at the mouth of the Suislaw River was assured when one William Moody set up a store in an Indian shack and started a post office in 1876, the year the Siuslaw Valley was opened to settlers. Before that time the land had belonged to the Siuslaw Indians but was gradually maneuvered away from them by treaties which as late as 1970 had not been honored by the United States government.

Interesting Sights and Places

An unusual nature study exhibit is the **Darlingtonia Wayside** five miles north of Florence. These exotic *Darlingtonia* plants, better known as cobra lilies, are carnivorous, trapping and eating live insects as part of the life support system.

Normally found in large bogs each side of the Oregon/California border, this particular area has been designated as a botanical preserve to allow interested persons to observe the large fields of the plants. Raised walkways in keeping with the natural environment are built through the fields of giant plants rearing their hooded leaves high from the root base for all the world like a nest of the snakes which have given them their popular name.

Display boards furnish illustrated information which explains the process by which these plants trap and digest small flying creatures.

Restrooms and a few picnic tables are part of the small wayside park, a short distance off Highway 101 on a paved street with well-placed directional signs.

Entering Oregon's world famous **Sea Lion Caves** is like moving into another universe. The caves, ranked among the most impressive of the earth's famous caverns, are compared frequently—perhaps inevitably—with the magnificent Blue Grotto of Capri.

The chamber is awesome: two acres of smooth stone surfaces and rock projections under a domed rock ceiling 125 feet high; its walls softly striped in muted grays and greens and sand tones and pinky-reds which mark off the ages, layer by layer, which comprised the earth's surface along the present shoreline; subsequently carved by the relentless action of the sea, working over milleniums, to this splendid cavern at the base of the 325-foot headland.

The nucleus of the cave is the great rock centered in the ocean pool, surrounded by tiers of tumbled stones. It is here that the families of stellar sea lions live—as many as 600 during the winter, tapering off to a few dozen during the warmer months.

These are the largest of the eared sea lions. Weighing around 50 pounds at birth, the bulls often grow to over a ton at maturity. The cows, much slenderer than the males, weigh up to 700 pounds each.

The large mammals have teeth and feed on fish, sometimes descending 600 feet into the ocean in search of food. They can forage underwater for periods up to five minutes before coming up for air. The animals live in harems of 15 to 20 cows to a senior bull on the ledges outside the caves during the summer months, breeding and giving birth there.

Because the cows desert the family structure easily, the herd bulls must maintain an around-the-clock alert against bachelor bulls eager to capture harems for themselves.

The animals are protected by law against killing or capture, and operators of the caves are careful to extend that protection to prevent disturbance by the thousands on thousands of visitors who come in to observe them in their natural environment every year. Observation areas, while offering unobstructed views of the sea lions, are not close enough to upset the creatures. Signs caution visitors to speak softly; cameras are allowed, but only without flash units. Maintenance and improvements are handled at times when there is no danger of upsetting the herds.

The caves were discovered in 1880 by a Captain William Cox who subsequently explored them by entering the cavern during calm weather in a small boat. Some years later he bought the land and the caves from the state, and it remained in his family's possession until 1927, when it was sold to a partnership for development as a tourist attraction.

A trail over a fourth of a mile long was constructed down the cliff face, ending in an enclosed wooden staircase which led to the northern entrance, and the caves were opened to the public in the fall of 1932.

The steep trail and the long staircase, while not dangerous, were forbidding in stormy weather. An elevator, begun in 1959, was completed in mid-summer of 1961 at a cost of $180,000. Since that time the caves have been operated as an all-year enterprise easily accessible to children and older persons, no longer restricted to adventurous parties willing to descend the outside trail to watch the animals at sea level.

The Indian Forest, as one might suspect, is a collection of replicas of authentic Indian dwellings set up in the forest four miles north of Florence. Forest paths lead through huckleberries and rhododendrons past full-sized reproductions of various types of Indian shelters: earth-mound lodge, plank long house, birch bark lodge, and others, in addition to the familiar pointed tipi. The dwellings are constructed to plans based on extensive research, and the development of the park is continuing as new houses are added.

The complex includes a small herd of buffalo also.

The **Indian Trading Post** at the entrance carries a wide selection of handmade Indian art: Navajo rugs and jewelry, Zuni beadwork, Hopi pottery, Kachinas, sand paintings, baskets, and moccasins. Souvenir-type items include hand-braided leather whips, "coonskin" hats, toys, and such.

Travelers will recognize the Indian Forest by the giant colored totem pole in front. The forest is open May through October. Hours for June, July, and August are 8 a.m. until dusk; for May, September, and October, 10 a.m. to 4 p.m.

Dolly Wares Doll Museum on Highway 101 just north of Florence has been around a long time—11 years to be exact. The doll collection has grown during that time to more than

2,500 dolls, many of them dressed in their original costumes. The oldest dates back to pre-Columbian times—a 4-inch clay figure. Some wooden dolls go back to the 17th Century.

The dolls come in all types and sizes: china and metal and celluloid dolls, wax and papier mache dolls, baby dolls and mama dolls and kewpies and Barbies—you name it, it's probably here. The largest is six feet tall. The smallest? Some dressed fleas—

Where do the dolls come from? Some are donated, others are purchased. Some are collected piece by piece and assembled at the museum. Present owner Sharon Smith, who has been at the museum over ten years, has the only repair and restoration facility for dolls in this part of the state, which is patronized by a large number of out of state customers.

"You have to outthink the manufacturer, the inventor, and the painter when you are repairing a doll," she says. Replacing glass eyes is the most difficult part of the restoration process. The best ones come from East Germany and are hard to get now; ones made in the United States are of inferior quality, Sharon feels.

She also custom dresses dolls to order, using clients' materials; and she can supply accessories for do-it-yourselfers such as wigs, shoes, and missing parts.

Doll collecting has grown in the last ten years until it is next to stamp collecting as the most popular "collector" activity. Reproductions of former doll favorites such as the Kewpie dolls of the 1920's is another current trend. Sharon has the original Skippy doll from which the molds were made for the recent reproductions of that once favorite toy.

Dolly Wares Museum is a fascinating place for adults and children alike—and children must be accompanied by an adult. But the charge is reasonable and cameras (without flash or tripod) are allowed in the well-lighted display hall. Hours are from 10 a.m. to 5 p.m. every day except Monday.

The Siuslaw Gallery of Local Arts is owned and staffed by a guild comprising 20 local artists. Since the opening in November of 1977, the Gallery has been an active contributor to community activities as well as serving as a showcase for the considerable collective talents of the members.

Changing displays of beach art, ceramics, jewelry, needlecraft, paintings, photography, and woodcrafts—both contemporary and traditional—are exhibited here.

The third week of May a "Spring Fever" exhibit is featured to coincide with the Rhododendron Festival held annually in Florence.

"Moonlight Madness" is a fun sale in October, complete with costumes, hot cider, and popcorn.

The "Anniversary Hoopla" in November commemorates the gallery's opening and signals the beginning of the annual Christmas Trinket Tree and Gift sale.

Siuslaw Gallery is easy to find in the lower level of the Siuslaw Pioneer Museum, one mile south of the Siuslaw Bridge on Highway 101. One of the members will be on hand to welcome visitors from 10 a.m. to 5 p.m. June through October; noon to 4 p.m. during the winter months.

The closest thing to the fountain of youth along the Oregon coast has to be **The Toy Factory**. From the outside the plain gray building doesn't appear to be a time-travel machine that transports adult visitors back into childhood with none of the startling side effects felt during takeoff in a 707 jet. But stepping through the door, senior citizens automatically begin to feel like Shirley Temples and Skippys. (Children, of course, are immune to this age-reversal process, holding multiple citizenship in the lands of *Now* and *Then* and *Happy Ever After* as they do.)

Sue Noel operates the store while husband Jim is busy in the factory turning out the novel games they have designed as the nucleus of their extensive stock of unusual toys. If anyone manages to get inside the shop without having made the magical transformation from grownup to child, her enthusiasm will take care of it on the spot.

This is strictly a DO TOUCH shop. "Here. Try it!" Sue laughs, demonstrating a *Flipperdinger* from the old-time toy collection manufactured in the Appalachian Mountains. "Or try the *Whimmydiddle*." In no time at all bystanders from 6 to 60 are operating a variety of simple folk toys. The effect is something like that of a kitchen band: a group of amateurs each doing his own thing in unison, wearing identical grins in assorted sizes.

Another such variety of original playthings will not be found south of Santa's workshop! There's something special about every toy in the shop. Puppets aren't just animated gloves at The Toy Factory. Stuffed fur skunks and beavers and raccoons come alive on small hands slipped inside these three-dimensional puppets from Pet Paws. And right on the counter at the back of the store is a basket of hand-knit finger puppets enticing visitors large and small to slip them on. (One size fits all.)

Wood toys are much in evidence: trains and planes and cars and stick horses, tractors and trucks (one with a carload of dominoes) line the shelves here, in lengths ranging from 2 inches to 2 feet. Imported, hand-crafted wooden carnival toys—a ferris wheel, an airplane swing, a carousel—are potential collectors' items. Jigsaw puzzles for younger children are made of polished wood: custom designs feature the letters of a child's name which fit into cut-out spaces on a panel faced with backing to keep them from falling through. A more elaborate sampler board has a cut-out alphabet, numbers from one to zero, and sliding counting beads. The Alpha Bag is a bag full of wooden letters, each individually cut and polished from pine. Extra letters can be ordered.

Kits of all sizes are for all ages (one table of items has a sign which reads TOYS FOR ADULT CHILDREN) are all over the place. Some that catch the eye: a Chinese Junk kit (wood) finishes up to 27" × 32", and it's a dream boat! "Little Trucks and Trains" kits, 4 to 5 inches long, are of wood with metal accessories but require no special tools for assembling, although younger children may need some help from parents for these. A plywood brontosaurus kit goes together without glue or fasteners and emerges 15" long when completed. The Blackmobil kit forms a geodesic sphere enclosing a crystal shape inside. The 30 pieces make a mobile 5 feet in circumference.

Sue and Jim believe that toys should be noncompetitive and involve participation. Among their designs is a marble juggler—a series of slanted chutes challenges the player to see how many marbles can be kept in motion by catching each as it comes to the bottom of the board and dropping it into the top, keeping several in the chutes at once. Easy? Well, the rules specify ONE HAND ONLY.

The Noels also make a version of the peg puzzles that grace restaurant tables across the country to keep diners occupied while waiting for their meals.

They supplement their own unusual toys with those made by craftspersons and small businesses, such as the folk toys described in Dick Schnacke's book, "American Folk Toys," from Mountain Craft Shop in West Virginia. Hand-crafted imports are all of superior quality here.

The shop includes one of the finest selection of books for young people ever found anywhere. Fiction of course, for entertainment; plus science books, manuals, picture books, and books for parents.

The Toy Factory is located just north of Florence on Highway 101. They are open noon to 5 p.m. every day (except during the winter they close during the middle of the week). Travelers going by are invited to stop in and play for awhile, and they'll go away with some stars in their eyes.

Fine Foods in Florence

Long-time vacationers in the Florence area remember the **Windward Inn**'s beginnings as a lunch counter and a gas station in the mid-1930's. It has evolved through a series of renovations to its present eminence as one of the finest restaurants not only on the Oregon coast, but in the state.

Van and Kathie Heeter, owners of the Windward Inn for the past 12 years, welcome guests "as a friend would welcome them into their homes." Stepping into the quiet charm of the Inn's dining areas, furnished with comfortable antiques in keeping with its "American Renovation" architectural style, diners can relax over excellent meals served with care.

The Windward Inn's menu is comprehensive to satisfy the tastes of almost anyone. The *Accompaniments* list includes both French fries and fresh sauteed mushrooms; you can order a luncheon of homemade pate, toasted bagel, fresh fruit and soup, or a hamburger; a pocket sandwich of chicken breasts and avocado, or a hot dinner sandwhich. And they'll all have one thing in common: each will be excellent in its own way.

Excellence is really the definitive word in describing the Windward Inn. Desserts and pastry are homemade every day; each pot of coffee is ground fresh; mussels are gathered daily by the staff from local beaches in season for their Sea Mussels Mariniers. A fine selection of wines is offered plus cocktail service during the dinner hour.

But it is the "littles" added to the excellent food that makes this the very special place it is. This is a FAMILY dinner house, and children are welcomed. Special smaller servings for "juniors and seniors" solve a real problem for those who can't eat large servings and dislike wasting fine food.

New recipes or seasonal foods are featured as daily specials. A traditional Merchant's Lunch is different every day. They will gladly accommodate special dietary requests. *Gladly* makes the difference.

The Florence branch of **Mo's** ("We aren't fancy but we're famous") is set up in an old cannery building on pilings out over the water on Florence's waterfront. There's a view of the graceful Siuslaw Bridge if you sit by the windows; otherwise the menu, the atmosphere, and the service are pretty much the same as the Newport originals.

The **Pier Point Inn**, Florence's on again-off again luxury convention center/motel complex is back in business and apparently intends to stay that way. Renovation of the six-year-old facility by the new management has brought it back to mint condition, ready to meet the city's need for a fine resort motel.

The dining room at the **Pier Point Inn** is terraced now to offer all diners a fine view of the Florence waterfront and stresses gourmet dining with an emphasis on seafood. A lounge and a coffee shop are also part of the motel complex.

Fisherman's Wharf in Old Town specializes in hearty food to delight fishermen and loggers. Breakfasts, served all day, are generous, featuring hotcakes the size of dinner plates, healthy portions of hash browns, and very good coffee.

Across from Fisherman's Wharf a small **Gazebo** set in a landscaped area overlooking the river, is a pleasant place for walkers and bikers to rest. A ramp nearby leads down to a dock where young and old come to sit and wait for the fish to bite.

A landscaped walk leads through a modern office complex and on to the old **Mapleton Depot,** moved a dozen miles downriver to its present site. It now houses an intriguing bookstore, **Train of Thought;** and **Antiquarian Gallery** which deals in rare prints and maps and other antiques.

Across the street from the Gazebo garden is the old **Kyle & Sons Building,** a Florence landmark for over 85 years. It houses **The Bay Street Steak and Noodle Co.,** a dinner house open evenings (except Tuesdays). Partners Bonnie Marx and Sharlene Nicholay have remodeled and redecorated the interior with antique furnishings and accessories to revive an early 1900's atmosphere. Menu items, including the homemade pasta which is their specialty, are under $5, except for steaks.

Up front the **Sand Dunes Frontier** appears to be one more attractive tourist enterprise offering a variety of fun activities: dune buggy rides, a trout lake, a miniature golf course, a game arcade, and a gift shop. Their advertising uses the same familiar adjectives tourists see and hear *ad infinitum*: "most beautiful," "outstanding," "the world's tallest, or first, or smallest—."

Private fishing ponds and mini golf courses are not unique along the coast; and gift shops are standard. But Sand Dunes Frontier has the first and best dune buggy game going, and that's what makes it special.

For there is no easy way to understand the awesome majesty of the dunes without experiencing them. Owners of private dune buggies are members of a select minority. For many of us, Sand Dunes Frontier offers an unusual opportunity to go deep into this natural wonderland to see and photograph the unbelievable panoramas.

This is a friendly place. Driver Ray McNair jokes as he help passengers—from tots to seniors—into his vehicle; and they make their own jokes as they choose their seats and fasten their seat belts.

But the moment the buggy enters the world of towering sand hills, silent except for the subdued growling of the engine as the vehicle follows shadow tracks along the contoured ridges, the riders become quiet too. It is as if they realize that the inflated adjectives cannot come near reality in describing the grandeur of the dunes.

McNair handles his cumbersome coach with the precision of a Mario Andretti, pushing up what appears to be sheer walls of sand, skirting precipitous curves and crevices, before dipping over the edge of one to grind down a 45-degree slope in low gear, the bloated tires laying twin furrows a yard wide behind him on the hillside.

The effect for the passenger is a little like taking a whirl on a 200-acre roller coaster. But McNair stops frequently to allow riders to catch their breaths and snap some pictures while he points out spectacular vistas which can only be seen from atop the sand mountains.

Small fresh water lakes are tucked away like emeralds in the folds at the bottoms of the steep valleys. From the high crests they appear as bonsai dish gardens, fringed by dark green conifers limned against rich sand tones with the spare perfection of oriental brush paintings.

Water in the lakes, 20 feet deep in some, stays fresh and good for drinking. They make excellent swimming holes on warm days. Air currents keep them from filling in, although the contours of the dunes themselves sift endlessly.

The golden sand billows as far as the eye can see—32,000 acres of it—(60,000 if you count the 35-mile stretch which underlaps the ocean along the shore line) centered here by the world's highest sand dune. At just under 400 feet it is taller than any in the Sahara. It is here the National Dune Buggy Association regional competitions are held annually, when as many as a hundred of the dune "bugs" wallow and grind through their paces on the massive sand mound.

For 25 minutes McNair steers the rumbling coach over the heights and valleys of the dunes, sometimes cutting new roads through the temperamental landscape that has shifted overnight to wipe out many of yesterday's trails. The ride, which on some of the steep climbs seemed to be lasting forever, suddenly is ending too soon.

Sand Dune Frontier operates the only commercial dune buggy rides in the Oregon Dunes National Recreation Area. Experienced drivers take visitors, who come from all over the world, into the desert-like expanses of wind-drifted hills and valleys of sand which resemble the great Sahara. Dune buggy excursions offer an intimate look at hidden lakes and remnants of buried forest while dipping and climbing the ever-changing sand formations. The excursions are offered the year around, weather permitting.

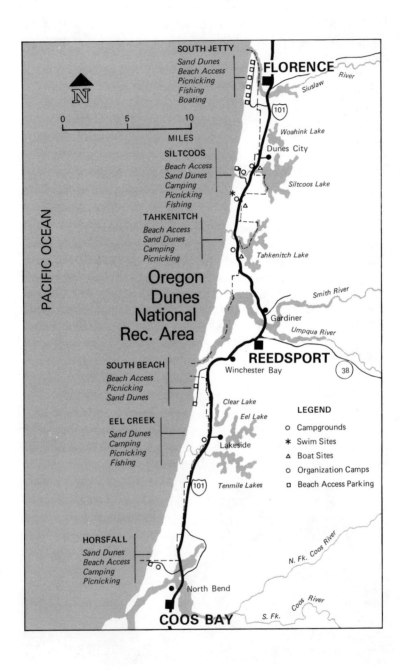

SOUTH JETTY
Sand Dunes
Beach Access
Picnicking
Fishing
Boating

FLORENCE

Siuslaw River

101

Woahink Lake

Dunes City

SILTCOOS
Beach Access
Sand Dunes
Camping
Picnicking
Fishing

Siltcoos Lake

TAHKENITCH
Beach Access
Sand Dunes
Camping
Picnicking

Tahkenitch Lake

PACIFIC OCEAN

Oregon
Dunes
National
Rec. Area

Smith River

Gardiner

Umpqua River

REEDSPORT

SOUTH BEACH
Beach Access
Picnicking
Sand Dunes

Winchester Bay

38

EEL CREEK
Sand Dunes
Camping
Picnicking
Fishing

Clear Lake

Eel Lake

Lakeside

LEGEND
○ Campgrounds
✳ Swim Sites
△ Boat Sites
◎ Organization Camps
▢ Beach Access Parking

101

Tenmile Lakes

HORSFALL
Sand Dunes
Beach Access
Camping
Picnicking

N. Fk. Coos River

North Bend

Coos River

COOS BAY

S. Fk.

0   5   10
MILES

N

As the driver assists the passengers from the buggy, it's obvious they had a good time on the excursion. A school boy wants to join another buggy, just pulling out, for a second trip. A grandmother announces she "wouldn't have missed it for the world—and would never go again!" The reactions of most of the riders seemed halfway between the two.

Myron Fullmer, owner of the buggies, says about 10,000 people a year take the dunes rides. This is a year-around activity, weather permitting, although 80 percent of the clients come in July and August. Buggies carry up to 20 people; more if children are held. There is no charge for youngsters under five who sit on parents' laps.

R. E. Chapman, owner/manager of Sand Dunes Frontier, once held title to the 240 acres of dunes wilderness adjacent to his roadside property. In 1972 it was absorbed by the government to become part of the Oregon Dunes National Recreation area, administered by the Forest Service. As the only commercial operator in the area, he must now pay fees for use of his former property. Rates are figured on a per person/per ride formula, which entails complex record keeping.

Chapman, who pioneered the dunes excursion trips on the central coast, also maintained a stable of horses for trail rides into the area until about two years ago. The numbers of private buggies in the area in recent years, plus escalating costs of caring for the animals through the winter, made it impractical to continue the operation. But Chapman gave it up reluctantly.

The neat 18-hole miniature golf course is popular with tourists. And children place the trout lake, where they can fish for a sure catch, high on their lists. The gift shop offers some interesting items—a collection of imported cups with charming bird designs from England is especially nice.

But it is the unique experience of entering the majestic sand dune wilderness that keeps visitors returning, and they come from all over the world. This is a stop the whole family will enjoy; one not to be by-passed. Sand Dunes Frontier is just beyond Honeyman Park, south of Florence, on Highway 101.

Woodsman's Native Nursery at 4385 Highway 101 on the north of Florence deals in plants and trees that grow naturally in the coastal area. The two-and-a-half acre nursery is owned by Lynn and Dale Center. For 10 years they have been supplying such items as huckleberry, salal, ferns, ceanothus, manzanita, Oregon grape, Port Orford cedar, Scotch broom and similar plants to nurseries around the country.

Another specialty is wild berry jams and jellies—huckleberry, blueberry, blackberry, and salal—homemade in the immaculate kitchen which is part of the modern building housing the garden shop. Each year more than a thousand gallons of juice are processed and frozen when the berries are in season and made in small batches as orders come in. And they come from all over the world. Gift packs hold four jars, one of each flavor, in four- or ten-ounce sizes and are postpaid in the continental USA. Customers may specify flavors and preferred shipping dates.

Floyd Doland, Jr. sees the Oregon coast from a different perspective than that of the average resident. Doland, operator of Seaplane Enterprises, has piloted scenic air flights over the central coastline for tourists and vacationers for the past 10 years. In the neat blue Cessna 180 (preferred choice of most Alaskan bush pilots), he gives his passengers a close-up of such landmarks as the lighthouse, the Sea Lion Caves, and sometimes an overview of migrating whales.

He comes from a flying family; both his mother and father were pilots, and Floyd had logged flight hours before he was out of high school. Five-and-a-half years in the Air Force and acquisition of a commercial pilot's license are supplemented by licenses which certify him for 100-hour plane inspections and flight instruction.

He also does aerial photography and recently flew a crew for a *National Geographic* project. And he works with Greenpeace to provide data on whale migration patterns.

Doland reports a change in responses from whales during the past couple of years. Formerly, he could fly over a group at 1,000 feet, and they would often breach and spout, apparently noticing the plane as a friendly object. Now when the plane flies over, they dive. He feels someone may have been shooting at them from a plane somewhere. He notes too that their northern feeding grounds have been disturbed in recent years, which may account for the increasing numbers of gray whales being seen along the Oregon coast the past few years.

The Dolands own 300 feet of Woahink Lake shore. At the present time they are converting part of it into a small woodland park with driftwood picnic tables and benches, and a fire pit, for use by friends and the Explorer Scout troop he leads.

The troop is in the process of converting an old Coast Guard boat into a replica of the *Santa Maria*, a long-term undertaking even with eight high school scouts spending most of their spare time on the project.

The Dolands are just setting up a shop which caters to proponents of self-sufficient lifestyles, which will carry such items as dehydrators, butter churns, grain mills, cider presses, and wood stoves plus a wide assortment of accessories.

Another sideline for him is finding burls of native woods which he seasons and slices into pieces for sale to crafts-people who manufacture clocks, tables, and sculptures from them.

Seaplane Enterprises is located four-and-a-half miles south of Florence near Woahink Lake Resort. The flights, scheduled for 15 minutes ($10 per person, with a minimum of two) are sometimes expanded to 25 minutes if there are more passengers. The rides are available the year around, weather permitting, except on Sundays.

The entire family will be fascinated by a stop at Seaplane Enterprises—and they will be welcome.

Annual Events

The annual **Rhododendron Festival** at Florence has an edge on other coast celebrations—about 73 years. But even after nearly three-quarters of a century of putting on the event each spring when the Rhodies bloom, it's still growing and improving.

You'd think after all that time there wouldn't be anything new in the way of activities to try, but each year finds some changes in the calendar of entertainment to attract the thousands of visitors who throng the town during the festivities. The first celebration held a parade, an athletic contest, a clambake on the beach, and a grand ball. That's four—well, five if you count the coronation of the queen—happenings. In 1979 there were 18 different activities, including races, parades, a puppet show, and band concerts: one by the Senior Citizens Kitchen Band, the other by the Eugene Highlanders Bagpipe Band (a traditional participant in the Rhody Festival for more than 25 years).

Since the first festival in 1908, Florence has elected a festival queen and staged a parade every year except for during World War I. And inevitably there is repetition: the first grand marshal of Florence's Rhododendron Festival was world renowned poet Joaquin Miller. In 1979 novelist Ken Kesey was grand marshal for the event.

GARDINER

Gardiner—the White City by the Sea—was established by crewmen of the shipwrecked *Bostonian* in October of 1850, the year the Territorial Legislature established 5,000 square miles of southern Oregon land between Roseburg and the coast as Umpqua County.

The *Bostonian* was one of three ships sent by San Francisco developers which were carrying supplies to expedite settlement of four new cities along the Umpqua River, the largest between the Columbia and San Francisco Bay. The developers, anticipating this would be the Northwest's shortest route to the gold fields of California, planned to establish **Myrtle Grove** at the head of tidewater (now Scottsburg), **Elkton** near the site of the Hudson Bay Company's Fort Umpqua, **Winchester** on the Oregon-California trail, and **Umpqua City** at the mouth of the harbor.

Most of the cargo from the wrecked ship was salvaged and carried nine miles north, and Gardiner's first buildings were erected. The town was named for the man who had piloted the *Bostonian* around Cape Horn. But it was W. J. Jewett, manager of the town's lumber mill—then as now its major business—who persuaded homeowners to paint their residences white, as those of his hometown in New England had been. Eventually every building in the community was so painted. Even today most are white, including the antique church with the bright red door on the bluff overlooking the town—the oldest mission still operating on the coast. A few newer houses along the highway at the edge of town flaunt bold colors, but they are few.

Terraced levels of a pioneer cemetery bank the hill across from the sprawling mill buildings which dominate the town. The elaborate headstones, moss-covered now inside the burial plots fenced with ornamental railings, bear dates in the early 1860's.

From the time it was built until the railroads came to the area in 1916, Gardiner was the industrial and cultural core of the region.

REEDSPORT/WINCHESTER BAY

Reedsport has been fighting a battle since its founding to keep its feet dry. The marshy ground on which it is built was flooded as often as not, and the original buildings and walkways were on stilts, as much as 8 feet above ground level, to keep them from flooding. Later the ground was filled in, and in the mid-1960's a dike was built to protect the town from the water.

Its sister city, Winchester Bay, is four miles southwest of Reedsport, but a road between the two was not completed until 1926. Together they form an entity which is the nucleus of the most popular sport fishing area on the coast. Winchester Bay was named for one of the original San Francisco developers of the Umpqua region in 1850.

The star attraction is Salmon Harbor, the largest (and certainly one of the most attractive) sport fishing marinas on the coast. There are 925 moorings in the harbor, about a third of them used by commercial boats. Also available are facilities for public boat launching, custom canneries, equipment rentals, scuba sales and service along with bait, fuel, and ice.

Salmon Harbor is self-supporting, operated jointly by Douglas County and the Port of Umpqua. Fees for moorage are figured at $10 per foot per year. Monthly fees are also based on size of the boat.

Several hundred overnight camping spaces for self-contained RVs rent at $4/night. Information is available at the modern office building at the entrance to the harbor.

Across the street from the harbor office is one of the most pleasant RV parks to be found anywhere. **Windy Cove Campground** is operated by Douglas County. The attractive park is protected by a hill, with lawns and trees and hook-ups, and is ideal for family vacation stays. Amenities include a store, a playground for youngsters, plus proximity to dunes and beaches. The old Coast Guard Station and the Umpqua Lighthouse State Park are located on the drive which curves to follow the beach past the state park campground. District Coast Guard buildings currently in use are at Salmon Harbor.

This is preferred territory for Chinook and silver salmon, found in ocean and river alike. Steelhead are plentiful in both the Smith River and in the Umpqua—the largest river flowing into the Pacific between the Columbia and San Francisco. The rivers also yield sturgeon, shad, perch, and Dungeness crab. Nearby lakes are known for rainbow trout, crappie, and bluegills. The area is truly a fisherman's paradise in variety and abundance.

Surfwood Campground and RV Park offers 141 sites with water, electricity, and some hook-ups. Additional conveniences include a fish cleaning area, showers, sauna, dump station, and store plus tennis, horse show, and shuffleboard courts and a heated pool. Play equipment signout is offered without charge. This attractive campground is on the east side of Highway 101 a half mile north of Winchester Bay.

A group of houseboats cluster near the bridge over the Umpqua River at Reedsport, complete with television antennas and clotheslines. The water-borne homes recall earlier days when the central town of Reedsport was built on stilts as much as eight feet above the ground to keep buildings from flooding.

In Reedsport's Old Town section, a visit to the **Reedsport Cheese Shoppe** is worthwhile. Although cheese is no longer manufactured at the site (local dairies cannot supply enough milk now to make it feasible), they are marketing the last cheddar made there, which has been aging for two-and-a-half years. They now purchase a basic cheese from nearby factories from which they concoct their natural whole milk flavored cheese. Noteworthy is an unusual cheddar (Trucker's Coffee) which is marbled with instant coffee.

In the spring the old brick building, painted white and fronted with a pink-and-white striped awning, looks rather like a gift package with two giant rhododendrons masquerading as pink bows. In addition to cheese (tasting is encouraged), they carry a selection of gift items which include cranberry sweets, wild berry jams, and goat's milk shaving soap.

Reedsport Cheese Shoppe is easy to find on Oregon Highway 38 one half-mile east of Highway 101.

Some excellent food is to be had at the **Harbor Light Restaurant** at the south end of the bridge, entering Reedsport. The driftwood gray exterior suits its locale. Owner G.A. Serang grew up on India's southern coast and brings a unique Indian emphasis to the rich varieties of seafood found in the Reedsport area. (To verify, try the shrimp sandwich with mild curry sauce, Serang's recipe, on a sourdough roll served with cole slaw and sprouts.)

Harbor Light is now open for dinner weekends until 8 p.m. The menu features seafood—15 original-recipe entrees adapted to American tastes. Prices: reasonable. Servings: generous. An eating experience you won't want to miss.

The office of the Oregon Dunes National Recreation Area, created in 1972, is located just south of the bridge on Highway 101. The 40-mile stretch of coastal dunes between Florence and Coos Bay—one of the largest in the world—is administered by the US Forest Service. The office, open weekdays, is an informational gold mine for vacationers and tourists.

The decline of dairy herds in the area has influenced the Reedsport Cheese Factory to close. The Cheese Shoppe in the old building is now a sales room for Oregon "gourmet" food items, plus their own specialty cheeses made from a cheese base purchased from regional factories and flavored to their own recipes. Customers are encouraged to stop by and taste the variety of cheeses offered and to browse for Oregon honey, jams, and other such regional items. Most unusual product offered is goat milk shaving soap.

Lacy steel scallops hang between concrete supports of the Yaquina Bay Bridge which spans the bay at Newport (above). The bridge and the Siuslaw Bridge (below) are two of the set of five coastal bridges completed during the 1930's depression under the Works Progress Administration (WPA).

The Bridges

A series of graceful bridges spans the major bays and rivers along the Oregon coast highway. The highway itself, begun in 1921, was conceived as a motor road following the coastline to be called the Roosevelt Military Highway. Prior to its construction sections of the beach served as roadways for vehicle travel and were passable only at low tide. It was completed in 1932.

Prime promoter of the project was Benjamin F. Jones, founder of the small community of Otter Rock north of Newport. He purchased the area for the site from one of the holders of a land allotment issued as replacement for tribal lands taken over by the government during the 1880's.

The concrete bridge across Rocky Creek near Whale Cove is named for Jones, "the father of the Oregon coast highway." The high, narrow arches anchor the span in a deep ravine visible from Otter Crest loop along a section known as "Ben's own wagon road" before it was incorporated into the highway constructed in the 1920's.

In January of 1934 $5,103,000 was designated for the construction of five coast bridges by the Works Progress Administration, the agency set up to create federal jobs during the 1930's depression by Franklin Delano Roosevelt. The five arched bridges were the final links in a hundred miles of central coast highway which opened the entire coastline as a major recreational and retirement area, easily accessible from inland valleys and neighboring states.

The **Yaquina Bay Bridge** at Newport was completed in 1936. The spans of the cantilevered bridge seem to tiptoe delicately across the bay, the large central deck arching almost 140 feet above the water to allow entrance of ocean-going freighters into the port area.

Waldport's **Alsea Bay Bridge** is a three-span cantilevered bridge, with a clearance of 70 feet, which carries traffic over the bay at the mouth of the Alsea River.

At Florence the **Siuslaw River Bridge**, the central one in the series, marches sturdily across the mouth of the Siuslaw River, supported by four thick concrete columns. These stolid underpinnings capped by dome headings resemble a quartet of medieval guardhouses from a distance.

The **Umpqua River Bridge** crosses the Umpqua River near Gardiner, close to its junction with Smith River, named for Mountain Man Jedediah Smith. The bridge is similar in design to its sister bridges—graceful steel spans on either side of a cantilevered archway.

McCullough Bridge at North Bend is the fifth WPA bridge. It is the longest—almost a mile—and the most expensive, with three suspension arches over the main channel supported on either side by a smaller concrete span. The channel spans clear 150 feet to accommodate ocean-going vessels. It is named for the designer of the bridges, C. B. McCullough, veteran bridge builder, and was dedicated June 5, 1936.

In an era when public sound equipment was just appearing on the American scene, some of the bridges were served at their dedications by one of the three Standard Oil Sound Trucks, which operated up and down the West Coast out of San Francisco at public gatherings for several years, in the same manner as the Goodyear blimps which for decades have floated above the crowds at public ceremonies around the country.

The Isaac L. Patterson Bridge, which crosses the Rogue River at Gold Beach, is named for the man who was Oregon's Governor from 1926 to 1929.

Thomas Creek Bridge north of Gold Beach is the highest bridge in Oregon. Rising 350 feet above ground level, it is higher than the Golden Gate Bridge—one of the world's longest bridges—with a span of less than a thousand feet.

Newest of Oregon's coastal bridges is the Astoria toll bridge, which crosses the Columbia River between that city and Megler, Washington—the world's longest continuous truss bridge, and the 16th in overall length (21,697 feet). Until the completion of the bridge in 1966, crossings were made by ferry.

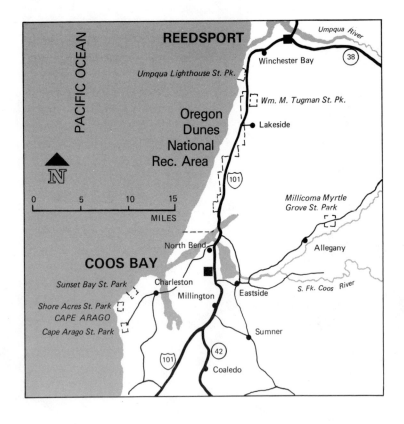

North Bend
Coos Bay
Charleston

NORTH BEND/COOS BAY

Coos Bay/North Bend is the world's largest shipping point for timber products. The first lumber was exported from the area in 1856, and two years later the brig *Blanca* came off the ways, the first ship built at the Simpson shipyards in North Bend.

The City of Coos Bay was originally named Marshfield by its founder, who raised the first structure there in 1854. It was incorporated as a city 20 years later; in 1944 the name was officially changed to Coos Bay.

North Bend, two miles to the north, was settled in 1853 and acquired by Asa Simpson in 1856, to become a company-owned town for Simpson mill and shipyard employees. In 1903 Louis Simpson, son of the founder, was instrumental in incorporating the city.

Interesting Things to See and Do

The Coos-Curry Museum in North Bend is a treasure chest of area history. But displays in the modern building in Simpson Park at the South end of the McCullough Bridge offer far more than antique furnishings and equipment. The usual array of furniture and china and tools and ornaments from an earlier day are preserved and presented there— among them a turn-of-the-century Regina Music Box, a hand-made spinning wheel, and the customary fine piano which had been shipped around Cape Horn.

But there is more.

Relics of the coastal area are represented by maritime artifacts such as the steering wheel from the *Roosevelt*, one of the freighters produced in the Simpson shipyards, which operated regularly between North Bend and Glasgow, Oregon for years. Also on display is an outstanding collection of 18 boat models handcrafted of inlaid wood by boat designer Frank Lowe, a joy to see and touch.

A delicate Chinese plaque inlaid with red, white, green and bronze jade on black lacquer which floated ashore from the freighter *Brush* when it broke up on Simpson Reef during a winter storm is especially lovely.

A comprehensive selection of Indian artifacts fills a section. Notable are aprons of intricate beadwork, one trimmed with small shells, the other decorated with 65 brass thimbles like a fringe of bells. Beadwork ceremonial robes are colorful and beautifully detailed. Baskets in an assortment of sizes and shapes, from two inches to two bushels, fill another corner. A stubby totem pole stands guard at a doorway near a fine collection of arrowheads said to be one of the best on the coast.

One unusual collection contains 59 slingshots, each one shaped by a local carver from a different native northwest wood. And in a special corner, seashore art of natural shells and driftwood is displayed in scenes which appear to be arrangements of hand-carved human and animal figures. An antique wooden leg supplies a humorous touch.

It's possible to buy a souvenir in the museum at small cost: tiny pieces of driftwood and miniature fossil rocks are on sale for under $1 each, for those who would like to take home a memento of the region.

Before leaving the museum grounds, visitors will want to investigate an old-time steam locomotive and other old logging equipment in the park nearby.

Exhibits of antique logging equipment are on display in Simpson Park adjacent to the Coos-Curry Museum, including the steam boiler shown here. The Museum is located at the south end of McCullough Bridge in North Bend. Collections include 59 hand-carved slingshots, each from a different native wood, and Indian beadwork.

The musuem is open every day except Monday. Hours May through September are 11 a.m. to 5 p.m. During the winter months the museum is open afternoons only.

CHARLESTON

The **Charleston Small Boat Basin**, nine miles west of downtown Coos Bay, lies just inside what experts describe as "the safest bar on the Oregon Coast." Deep sea fishing is excellent. Charleston Charters (888-4846) and B&B Charters (888-4139) operate out of the harbor on a daily schedule. Tackle is furnished for both salmon and bottom fishing. Necessary licenses are available at the charter offices; nearby cafes pack fishermen's lunches; dock area canneries will freeze, smoke, or can catches for transportation home. Reservations are required.

Here at Charleston is located the **Marine Biology Institute of the University of Oregon**. And on South Slough just past the basin the **Estuarine Sanctuary** is maintained for the preservation of coastal wildlife.

The sanctuary is one of seven in the United States which were established under the Coastal Zone Management Act of 1972. These estuaries (places where fresh and sea waters merge) are still in their natural states. They provide protection not only for the marine environment but for all wildlife found there. In South Slough this includes birds, small marsh creatures, and large animals such as deer and elk.

Protection takes many forms: discouraging hunting, and promoting the use of nonpowered water craft there rather than the use of power boats, for instance. The overall effort is directed toward preserving the area in its natural state as much as possible.

The sanctuary at the southern tip of Coos Bay contains 6,000 acres of woods and marshes and 600 acres of water. Scientists and students hope to inventory the region's wildlife. Environmentalists, sportsmen, and other interested groups are invited to visit the sanctuary as part of the extensive wildlife educational program being developed by the staff.

Funds for the South Slough site were provided by a combination of federal, state, and donated money. The Estuarine Sanctuary is administered under the State Lands Division.

Research now being followed at the South Slough site and at others in the program will be used world-wide in the development and management of estuaries.

Wood 'N Things near the entrance to the boat basin houses a quality selection of regional and imported gifts. Co-owner Jeanne Freshwater (with husband Al) says prices range from $500 to 10$^¢$. Outstanding are exquisite pottery in delicate shades of blue by Virginia Morgan; fine porcelains by Spanish designer Lladro; and for collectors, hard-to-find ivory netsukes—hand-carved replicas of ancient small animal lucky pieces. Also notable: prints by Dan McMichael; limited edition silkscreen prints by Wendy Morgan; boxed notecards featuring Elton Bennett prints. Definitely a DO STOP shop!

Three State Parks

An intermeshing system of state parks near Charleston provides one of the most attractive combinations of facilities and recreational activities anywhere on the coast. Among them they offer excellent camping, picknicking, and accommodations surrounded by scenic and outdoor fun areas unique in number and interest. And, except for the modest charges at overnight camping spots, all are available without charge. This is a fine location for a summer vacation in the old tradition of settling down for a week or two to enjoy the serenity and beauty of lazy days by the ocean.

Sunset Bay State Park is just that—a parkland providing both tent and trailer facilities in sheltered spaces which allow plenty of privacy. Excellent utility buildings are clean and convenient, with both laundry and shower accommodations for campers. Water and firewood are standard here.

Large covered shelters house electric stoves and other conveniences for group cookouts, with picnic tables close by. Cleaning tables are located in central areas for easy handling of the abundant catches anglers enjoy here. Sunset Bay golf course is part of the park system. The jewel-like Sunset

Beach deserves its world-wide reputation for charm and beauty. It is sheltered by cliffs which are broken just enough to form a narrow sea channel, making it one of the calmest of the coast beaches.

Shore Acres a short way up the road looks like the setting for an episode of the old *Bonanza* TV series. Its story reads like one. Embracing 1,000 acres of wildly beautiful Oregon coastline, this is the site of the coastal empire developed by California shipping magnate Lewis J. Simpson during the first half of the century.

Bounded on the north by South Bay, a delightfully secluded cove beach, the forested acres rise dramatically to the grandeur of Cape Arago, the headland which shelters the small harbor where Sir Francis Drake may have made his only landing during his exploration along the north Pacific coastline. The heart of the holdings, where the Simpson mansion once sat among acres of formal gardens, is guarded by monolithic cliffs carved by tides which send lashings of spray over the top of the 75-foot promontory when coastal gales are blowing.

Simpson's father, Asa, came to California in 1849 to bring supplies to miners during the gold rush. Within 10 years he had acquired timber holdings along the Pacific Coast north of San Francisco, establishing shipyards at Coos Bay, Oregon, and Gray's Harbor, Washington, from which more than 50 ships were produced to sail the world's oceans. Beginning in 1859 with the two-masted brig *Blanco*, his output increased during the next 20 years to include regular manufacture of four-masted vessels. In 1888 the first five-masted ship produced on the Pacific Coast was built at the Coos Bay yards—the schooner *Louis*.

His other business enterprises included lumber mills, logger operations, a fleet of freighters, and a packet service which linked Portland and San Francisco with regular runs.

Louis Simpson came to Oregon in 1899 to manage his father's interests and began development of the town of North Bend. He bought the central 320 acres of the estate in 1905 for $4,000 from a white settler who had recently lost his

Oriental gardens surround a sunken pool, centered by bronze herons, at the south end of four acres of formal landscaping which once embraced the mansion at Shore Acres, the elegant estate of West Coast shipping magnate Lewis J. Simpson. The gardens contain plantings from around the world, many brought from far countries in the sailing ships manufactured in the Simpson shipyards at North Bend. The gardens are maintained as a part of the state park system.

Indian wife. Playing on the man's loneliness, he negotiated the deal and began clearing the land the next year. In 1907 construction was begun on the fabled mansion, the largest house in Oregon in its time. A Christmas present for his wife, the mansion was used as a summer home until 1914, when a 75-foot addition added a ground floor bath house with a $26' \times 52'$ swimming pool, bedrooms on the second floor, and a full-length ballroom on the third level.

In July of 1921 the house and contents, sadly under-insured, were destroyed by fire, a catastrophe which under-mined the Simpson fortune beyond recovery. Simpson moved into a small house on the estate from which he con-ducted his business. In 1923, salvaging lumber from one of his own schooners wrecked on Simpson's Reef off Shore Acres, he began construction of a second home—a ranch house 225 feet long—to be built by a Swedish contractor from plans drawn by a local draftsman. More informal than the first, the 17-room house surrounded by its formal gardens served as the center of the coastal estate. A nearby cove provided a private beach with picnic tables and bath houses; to the south were located a smaller ranch house and barns for the manager in charge of the herd of Simpson cattle which grazed the headlands of Cape Arago.

In the early 1930's Simpson donated 135 acres of his land to the State of Oregon for Cape Arago State Park. Ten years later the Simpson fortune, all but gone, could no longer support the luxurious estate, and Louis Simpson sold the re-maining 637 acres of his Shore Acres property to the State for $29,000. The residence became a clubhouse for members of the tank batallion stationed at Cape Arago during World War II.

By 1948 the maintenance of the property had become too costly for the State of Oregon to justify, and the mansion was razed, except for the dining room wing which was moved and now serves as the garden cottage. Three years later the carriage house was also demolished.

But the magnificent botanical gardens, with plantings brought from all over the world by the Simpson ships, are maintained as a part of the Oregon State Park system. In spite of severe damage during the Columbus Day storm in 1962, the gardens today are open the year around for public enjoyment.

Winding walkways entice viewers into hidden dells, past the sunken oriental pond rimmed with plantings ranging from azaleas to palm trees which frame sculptured bronze herons whose graceful shadows are mirrored in the still surface of the water. Unsuspected clearings could serve as fairy courtyards in the moonlight; they are reached through shadowy wooded glens which undoubtedly harbor elves. One irresistible path scrambles along the cliff tops like a frisky tomboy to the topmost point of Cape Arago.

There is no charge for enjoying the magnificent vistas, the splendid gardens, the sense of freedom one feels while standing in the wind on the cliff searching out the horizon line where sea and sky merge. Picnic tables and benches are placed in sheltered spots. It is not unusual to come upon a wedding in progress against the background of azaleas and rhododendrons.

And it is easy to reach by turning off Highway 101 at Coos Bay to the Charleston Boat Basin, then following the coast road around past Sunset Beach as it rises to the entrance of the Shore Acres estate. Viewpoints offer glimpses of the Cape Arago Lighthouse and an overview of Simpson's Reef, one of the most dangerous points for Pacific Coast sea traffic along the Oregon coastline.

Shore Acres is not a place to visit in a hurry. This majestic coastal panorama created over the ages by the relentless action of winds and tides seems to reduce time measured by minutes and hours to its proper proportions in relation to history.

Cape Arago is a place of wild beauty, evolved over fifty million years by tidal activity whittling away at the shoreline. The spectacular results are sculptured sandstone bluffs unlike any others along the coast. Waves crashing against these inverted cliff formations are churned to a frothy white which turns the ocean to whipped cream around the roots of the great walls.

The winds blow over the small grassy headland atop Cape Arago as if determined to sweep it clean of intruders who insist on visiting this unprotected area. But the wide-angle view offered from the promontory with its small historical monument includes a glimpse of the tiny cove which—who knows—may have once provided harbor for Drake's *Golden Hind.*

Easy Shopping

North Bend is home for the southwest coast's largest shopping center, **The Pony Village Mall**, which provides most services the average shopper would expect to find under one roof. The Mall, adjacent to the **Pony Village Lodge**, also features weekly events which include art and photography shows, and other community activities.

While there, take time to stop by **Cone 9**, a kitchen shop worth browsing. Look for the unusual facade while strolling the mall: brick walls without mortar are held in place by timbered door and window frames in an arch pattern. Inside are some unusual gourmet cooking items—individual pottery molds patterned in brown and white designs are especially attractive. They also carry a good assortment of pasta equipment such as ravioli pans, and cutting machines adjustable to several widths; and a wide selection of iron cookware—corn stick pans, egg poachers, oversized dutch ovens and such, in addition to skillets in all sizes. Clever small items include clear plastic boxes by the dozens in soft rainbow colors, ranging from one-inch square to 5 × 8 inches. Tea cozies of fake sheepskin have appliqued features which make them look like the real McCoy.

The Earring Tree glitters, literally, from jewelry covering the walls and hanging in shimmery cascades from high racks which fill the room's center. The stock is varied, ranging from inexpensive costume pieces to diamond-and-gold items. Some "specials" include jeweled combs, crystal mobiles, interesting bronze and pewter belt buckles; and a pendant novelty— names rendered in classic Egyptian hieroglyphs in gold-tone metal, thumb-nail size, and priced in the "teens." Owner Bun-

Cape Arago is an area of great sandstone cliffs which seem to lean out over the ocean which beats against their footings in relentless lashings.

ny Estes of **The Seaweedery** has gathered some lovely and unusual items in her small shop. Interspersed among gifts which include wall-plaque owls crafted in feathers, and macrame (lampshades, and a spectacular display shelf hanging trapeze style from a ceiling beam) are plants and flowers and baskets. Hidden around a corner is a 3×4-foot driftwood ship's model with full rigging. Delightful background music is furnished by three canaries and four parakeets in bamboo cages imported from mainland China, charming enough to be used as hangings in their own right.

Down at the end of the mall and around a corner is **Captain Bly's**, a seafood deli with a near-lifesized wooden pirate standing guard outside the open-front dining room. Seascape murals cover the walls. Clients can choose from an assortment of seafood delicacies and enjoy them at the plank tables or take them out.

The Coos Bay Mall is a four-block section of modern shops fronting on Bayshore Drive, the landscaping still young enough to have a fragile appearance without looking skimpy. This inviting shopping area is centered by a wide mall, flanked by ample parking spaces.

The **On Broadway Theater**, Coos Bay, started as a showcase for local talent via vaudeville-style theater alternating with the showing of film classics. The On Broadway now is home base for a company of performers—The Dolphins—which presents year-round theater ranging from standard comedy and drama to original material such as the one-hour one-woman show, "Metamorphosis," written and performed by area actress Bennii Worthington.

The Little Theater on the Bay, Virginia and Washington, North Bend, stages frequent productions throughout the year.

Recommended Restaurants

The Portside—elegant dining overlooking the Charleston Boat Basin—features fine seafoods. Reservations suggested.

The Pony Village Lodge dining room—a full restaurant facility for breakfast, lunch, and dinner.

Leave by the Back Road

The Seven Devils Road is a beach loop drive which takes travelers through charming rural countryside between Charleston and Bandon. The paved road is narrow in places and winds through the forested hills between Highway 101 and the shore. The drive offers access to three of the best "rock combing" beaches to be found along the coast: **Whiskey Run**, **Merchant's**, and **Agate** beaches. Stones of brilliant colors are abundant on all three of the beaches along with agates and jasper.

The road 10 miles or so in length, rejoins Highway 101 just before it crosses the Coquille River north of Bandon.

Annual Events

The **Haydn Festival**, Coos Bay, in early August.

The **Annual Orchid Society** display and the annual orchid auction in early December.

Doug Wilson displays two black rockfish and a ling cod caught from a rocky shore along the Oregon coast near Depoe Bay with new lures.

Catching More Bottom Fish

Here in the Pacific Northwest and along the Oregon Coast, anglers have access to a great many bottom species from small perch and flatfishes to large rockfishes in the 20-pound class. Ling Cod attain weights in excess of 60 pounds. Pacific Halibut reach 200 pounds. Many species may be taken on gear ranging from ultra-light spinning gear to wire-line-rigged boat rods.

For years the glamorous (and tasty) salmon and steelhead trout have overshadowed the bottom fish along Oregon's coast, bays, and estuaries. But salmon and steelhead trout are migratory and seasonal. They are also more difficult to catch for most anglers.

Bottom fish offer an alternative fishing challenge. They are available at all seasons of the year, eagerly attack a variety of lures and bait, are sporty on the right tackle, and are absolutely delicious on the table. Despite the availability of bottom fish all along Oregon's coast and salt-water inlets and bays, many anglers lack the know-how to consistently catch bottom fish. Many bottom fish may be caught accidentally while searching for salmon. But, when these same fishermen use new techniques and specially designed lures, they can enjoy hours of great fishing pleasure and an appreciation of the sport that bottom fish can provide when taken on tackle matched to the fishing conditions and the types of fish taken.

Many bottom fish are still caught using herring and salmon-style hookups, primarily because most fishermen seek bottom fish the same way they mooch for salmon. But, a fantastic breakthrough in bottom fishing techniques has evolved from research. These techniques, new to Oregon coast waters, use leadhead jigs and plastic worms. They will amaze even dedicated bottom fishermen who have been using standard bait or jigging techniques. Originally developed for freshwater bass fishing and refined from jigs with pork rind, the leadhead jigs and plastic worms provide an entirely new approach to shallow-water bottom fishing.

This method is so effective that it has been used extensively in Puget Sound by the National Marine Fisheries Game Fish Project and Washington State Fisheries to collect bottom fish for tagging studies. More recently the Seattle Aquarium has been using shallow-water fishing techniques with leadhead jigs and plastic worms to collect display fish.

Black Rockfish are frequently found in schools feeding on or near the surface. A light steelhead rod or bass casting rod with jigs will bring strikes so fast and furiously you'll be wondering why you've never found the fish like this before.

Fishing early in the morning we have run into schools of surface-feeding Blacks. With both of us casting, we stayed constantly hooked up to fish for 30 minutes before we wore out our wrists landing and releasing Blacks as fast as we could cast and land them.

The secret to our success was simple—knowledge of proper rockfish habitat and lures that yield the greatest efficiency in fishing results. While salmon are fast-moving fish that charge through baitfish, more rockfish tend to lie in wait and make a short dash to grab the unsuspecting prey. Black and Yellowtail Rockfish do feed on small herring; however, they and other rockfish ambush their prey from close range.

By concentrating on shallow-water fishing, we've found that we can easily catch whatever fish we want to for our table, have more fun doing it, and are frequently able to go fishing more often by taking shorter but very productive trips. Bottom fish can be close at hand if you study the shoreline.

In slinging ¼-ounce jigs and plastic worms from the rocky shoreline at Depoe Bay, we found that we could land hard-running Blue Rockfish, a fish often mistaken for Black Rockfish. We were using light spinning tackle and waiting for the waves to help us lift our fish up to the rock ledge where we could land them. We were hooking and landing the Blues and Ling Cod within 100 feet of US Highway 101, the main street of this small fishing community—famous for salmon and bottom fishing charters. The area offers many miles of shoreline fishing possibilities. If you are traveling to the coast and your schedule does not permit time to go fishing by private or charter boat, don't overlook the opportunities for shore fishing. When we spotted the section of the rocky shoreline which obviously was several feet deep right at the water's edge, we knew that we had a likely spot. We quickly confirmed it by hooking a fish on the second cast. Enough action followed in the next half hour to provide several fish dinners.

We've fished plastic worm-leadhead jig combinations from cartoppers, piers and jetties, shoreline, and in the open ocean all along the Oregon coast. Jigs and plastic worms outfish bait on shallow-water rockfishes at least 5 to 1. The secret seems to be the curly-tailed plastic worms! The undulating tail movement of the worm adds that ingredient that must spell FOOD in capital letters to the hungry rockfish waiting for his next morsel to swim along.

The best part about fishing with these jigs is—if you already own a medium-weight mooching or steelhead rod and reel capable of casting these light jigs or even your lightweight tackle used for trout fishing, you've got everything you need except the jigs—to catch more fish and have more fun.

Doug Wilson
Fred Vander Werff

Doug Wilson and Fred Vander Werff are authors of "New Techniques for Catching Bottom Fish" and manufacture the unique leadhead jigs and plastic worms used as lures. For a price list of lures, write Sebastes Fisheries Company, P.O. Box 310, Kirkland, WA 98033.

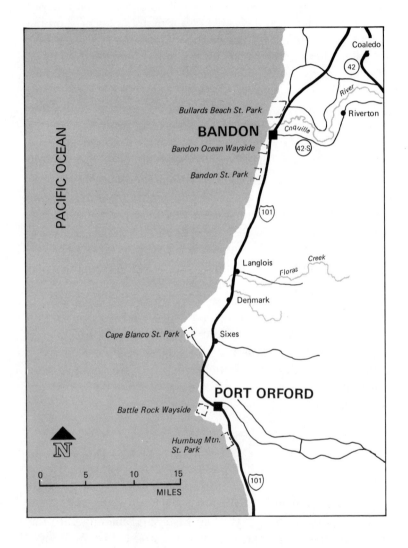

Coaledo

42

River

Riverton

Bullards Beach St. Park

BANDON

Coquille

42-S

Bandon Ocean Wayside

Bandon St. Park

PACIFIC OCEAN

101

Langlois

Creek

Floras

Denmark

Cape Blanco St. Park

Sixes

PORT ORFORD

Battle Rock Wayside

N

Humbug Mtn.
St. Park

101

0   5   10   15

MILES

101

Bandon
Port Orford

BANDON

Bandon is the Cranberry Capital of Oregon—one of five states to grow cranberries. For most of us cranberries are "something extra" to spice up holiday dinners at Thanksgiving and Christmas, but in Bandon they are a year-around business. Roughly 900 acres of this native American fruit are in cultivation in Bandon area bogs.

The major supply of the world's cranberries come from their original locales: Massachusetts, New Jersey, and Wisconsin in the East, and Oregon and Washington in the Pacific Northwest. A few are grown in the Canadian provinces of Ontario, Quebec, and British Columbia; and on the island of Terschelling in Holland which produces 125 tons yearly from vines started when a barrel of raw fruit was scattered there during a shipwreck and allowed to grow wild.

Cranberries demand an acid peat base soil and as a result are confined to areas where these natural bog bases are found. Northern Oregon cranberries are grown on peat bogs up to 30 feet deep which were producing wild berries when Lewis and Clark first traded with the Indians for them in November of 1805.

Cultivated cranberry vines were imported from Massachusetts in 1879 by pioneer grower Charles McFarlin from which was established the parent strain for most cranberries grown on the coast today. But settlers homesteading on the Clatsop Plains were shipping them to California settlers before that time.

From the small bogs planted by McFarlin, cleared with shovels and hand-picked by members of the Coos Indian tribe, the areas' production of cranberries has grown to 400,000 pounds of processed berries a day at the height of the harvest, a sizable percentage of the national crop. Modern equipment (much of it designed in the Bandon area) and the use of irrigation, plus the development of hybrid strains especially suited to the northwest climate, have placed Oregon cranberries at the top of the scale among processors. Noted for their deep rich ruby color, they are in demand for mixing with paler eastern varieties to enrich the color of commercial cranberry juice.

Oregon coast cranberry growers have borrowed from the lumber industry in developing efficient harvesting methods. With the water reel (a machine designed for wet picking) the bogs are flooded and the reels rotated to agitate the water surface with enough force to shake the berries from the vines. They then float to the surface and are pushed by long booms toward a submerged hopper in the same way logs are manipulated toward the mill belts. Conveyors then lift them to trucks.

An alternate method of wet harvesting is to pump the berries directly into the waiting trucks, where the water drains out through the tailgate. Wet picking harvest is used for 85 percent of the Oregon harvest.

Dry picking is handled by a vacuum machine equipped with forks which lift the berries off the vines and onto a belt from which they are bagged for hauling.

Part of the bog workers' gear is unique: stilt shoes made by fastening wooden platforms with short wooden pegs to the soles of their boots, enabling them to walk through the vines without trampling the berries.

Cranberries are harvested in the late fall. **Ocean Spray Cranberry** company at Bandon processes more than 90 percent of the cranberries grown in the state.

In late September Bandon hosts its annual festival complete with the usual trappings: a parade, the coronation of a queen, and a barbeque in the park. A Cranberry Fair is held in conjunction with the festival where local ladies bring homemade cranberry foods for sale: jams, breads, cakes, candy, and more.

Tours of local cranberry bogs are encouraged during the harvest season when the "crimson ponds" are at their most colorful. The Chamber of Commerce in Bandon coordinates the trips. Tours of the Ocean Spray processing facilities may be arranged, subject to seasonal conditions, by contacting the company offices in Bandon.

Cranberries, harvested in late fall, float to the surface of the flooded bogs and are pushed by large rakes. About 900 acres of cranberry bogs are cultivated in the Bandon area, the cranberry capital of Oregon. Oregon cranberries are especially prized by commercial canners for their deep red color.

Interesting Things to See and Do

A visit to the **Coquille Valley Dairy Co-op** at the northeast end of Bandon on Highway 101 offers an opportunity to see at first hand the operations which go into the making of world-famous Bandon cheddar cheese. New state health laws prohibit tours of cheesemaking plants, but the factory at Bandon has the large viewing window now common to cheese factories where viewers can watch the processes by which milk becomes cheese. A narrated color slide presentation fills in with other information.

A salesroom at the factory is open from 8 a.m.-5 p.m. Monday through Saturday. As in all five Oregon cheese factories, salespeople here will gladly wrap and mail gift purchases for customers.

The **State Fish Hatchery** a mile east of Bandon on the highway is one of 32 operated by the Oregon Department of Fish and Wildlife throughout the state. These hatcheries are maintained to supplement game fish in Oregon waters, mainly with salmon, steelhead, and trout. Visitors are encouraged to tour the installations and view the procedures here.

From Bandon's Old Town the **Beach Loop Road**—several miles of scenic secondary highway—ambles through a rural countryside of small farms that seem to have survived intact from a quieter era.

Some parts of it have survived for eons. The beaches are studded with great rock formations, remnants of a prehistoric coastline. **Face Rock**, a giant carving shaped by the battering tides, resembles the head of a sleeping man, for instance.

Fields of sandy coast land are covered with waving shore grass which in early spring is frosted with hazy blue, infiltrated by invading hordes of wildflowers.

Misty Meadows, a small shop whose stock in trade is homemade jams, is located above Myrtlewood factory near the Bandon end of the loop. The name is appropriate.

Windermere Inn—a landmark resort on the southern Oregon coast for many years, is literally a stone's throw from an interesting beach. All units have kitchens. There are queen-sized beds, and NO PHONES. And pets are welcome. This is a truly delightful setting for leisurely family vacationing.

There are stopping places along the way from which to view the abandoned lighthouse, a small square white toy building on the tideflats below the road which would be more at home on Eugene Field's Land of Counterpane. Yellow Scotch broom covering the hilly road heights makes a lovely frame or color photographs of the tiny light station at the mouth of the Coquille River, a landmark since 1896.

The road follows a long lovely beach before rejoining Highway 101. It is a perfect route for hikers or bikers. The state wayside area on the beach offers easy access to fishing, beachcombing, and a most lovely view while picnicking.

West Coast Game Park is a treat for old and young alike. There are few fences here. The deer roam the park at will, as do sheep and goats; and there are exotic animals from around the world. This walk-through zoo encourages children to pet the livestock. And there are no DO NOT FEED THE ANIMALS signs in evidence; quite the contrary. Over 350 birds and animals are here to be observed close up in a natural setting. Adventurous kids of all ages can take a ride on a water buffalo; for those less daring there are pony rides.

This "walk-through safari" seven and a half miles south of Bandon is an experience most visitors to the area won't want to miss.

Quality Shops

Old Town Artisans, the group of highly skilled crafts-people who have located their studios along First Street opposite Bandon's dock area, represents one of the most varied and interesting consortiums of artisans to be found in one location along the Oregon coast. Their works include pottery, sculpture, stoneware, and porcelain; hand-crafted jewelry, stained glass, and weaving.

Westerly Webs weaving studio, kitty-cornered from the Bandon Fisheries warehouse, is a wonderland for weavers, knitters, and macrame artists. Hanks of colored yarns dangle in rainbow bundles from the ceiling beams; hangings woven from hand-spun fibers combined with driftwood show to perfection against the rough plank walls. Racks of hand-woven, hand-knit vests, sweaters, and ponchos by local designers appeal to the most discriminating shopper at prices which are far more moderate than the quality suggests.

Bins of wools and craft necessities are tempting to crafters. Westerly Webs is "the only shop in the world to feature myrtlewood weaving accessories"—things of beauty in their own right without considering their utilitarian qualities. Open cubicles on the back wall are stuffed with imported and specialty yarns, including those spun from the fleece of the area's flocks, prized by big-name manufacturers of rugged outdoor sweater jackets.

An adjunct room holds looms of various sizes and complexities. Assorted spinning wheels are silhouetted in the wide store-front window against an ocean view.

Joyce Farr, Wilma Myers, and Nola Smith, experts in their field, offer individual instruction and hold classes for weavers and spinners who come from all over the Northwest to participate. Special short-term classes are offered during the summer to allow vacationers to take full advantage of one or two weeks of instruction. This is also the meeting place for the Humbug Mountain Weaver's Guild, and interested guests are welcome to attend meetings on the second Thursday of each month from 10 a.m. to 3 p.m.

The West First Street Studio is located where First Street turns sharply right and left again toward the jetty. Gary Ekker (stoneware and porcelain) and Bernie Dalmazzo (bronze sculpture) have removed the inside partitions of an old dock-area building to convert it to an indoor Japanese Zen garden as a setting for their work. Rocks, plants, and ripple-raked sand in harmonious arrangements are supplemented by hand-crafted benches to provide areas for contemplation. Light from fixtures in the high-raftered room filters through bamboo screens. Hours are irregular, but it's worth taking a chance on finding these artisans at home.

In the same square block, but facing Second Street, are located the **Bandon Art Glass Studio** and the **Whiskey Run**

Silver Shop. Stained glass artist John Campbell and Silversmith George Gaspar share a studio/shop which resembles the inside of a treasure chest. The windows are a patchwork of stained glass pieces so that the light inside has a rainbow quality. Along one side, glass-topped show cases sparkle and gleam as the light plays over Gaspar's jewelry and gem collections.

Gaspar, who does his own lapidary work as well as the metalsmithing, combines semiprecious gems with silver and gold in truly imaginative forms to produce jewelry that is wearable as well as striking. His collection of picture jasper is interesting in the larger pieces; smaller cuts made into rings and pendants are hauntingly lovely. The natural scenes and figures from the half gems are almost unbelievable in their life-like appearances. Birds, flowers, landscapes have the look of hand-painted miniatures, exquisite in coloring and proportions.

John Campbell's workroom at the back of the shop is as fascinating as Gaspar's jewelry area. Campbell, whose works are commissioned from all over the United States, produces stained glass pieces which range from small plaques to murals and are stunning in color and design. It's worth a trip to the studio just to browse through his portfolio of completed works. And it is pure pleasure to watch the precision with which he handles his fragile materials. Truly, Bandon Art Glass features "stained glass in the tradition of Renaissance artisans."

Before leaving, visitors should look over the Copper Frog Pond display of handmade copper frogs by Claud Whaley in one corner of the shop. These delightful small sculptures depict a family of frogs doing "people things." They are not replicas cloned from a few designs; like the humans they emulate, each Whaley frog is made individually and each expresses Whaley's pixie humor in its own way.

Gaspar and Campbell display products of other local craftspeople which are compatible with their own quality works.

Hidden away near the end of First Street, which ends at

the jetty, is **Western Heritage Books**. L.V. and Eloda Blickenstaff, both retired, established the Bandon business six years ago after moving to the area. Their specialty is out-of-print books, and as with many selective services such as this one, word-of-mouth advertising from pleased customers has promoted their book business into a year-around, six-day-a-week enterprise with clients all over the world.

The Blickenstaffs also sell fine antique glassware and china; and they carry collectables for those who are looking for mementos.

Nor are all their books out of print. They also sell current releases, and visitors are invited to browse for books or antiques any day but Monday, when they're closed.

The shop is in a green shake building on Beach Loop Road overlooking the abandoned lighthouse—tiny as an accessory piece for a model railroad layout seen from the hill.

Coming into Bandon proper, Highway 101 makes a sharp left turn, then a few blocks later turns right again, splitting off of Second Street which leads down to the jetty. Within this area are located several shops which carry a wide variety of merchandise which has been around for years but still has plenty of life left.

On the same side of the highway, about halfway between the two corner turns, the **Bandon Flea Market** offers "trivia and nostalgia" items as well as antiques. Owners Bill and Karen Smith also have tables to rent to those who wish to bring their own items to the Flea Market for sale.

Still on the left side of the road and straight ahead on Second Street where the highway turns toward Port Orford, is Brian Vicks' **Neat Old Stuff**—American antiques and collectables.

Around the corner of First Street, and down a way is **Hand Me Down Kate's**, a secondhand clothing store that is worth looking into. "Vintage goods" is the way these still usable items are described by owner Catharine Shindler.

Zumwalt's Myrtlewood Factory seems more like a myrtlewood variety store, although many of the items are indeed manufactured by the owners. The inventory includes a basic stock of myrtlewood tableware supplemented by special pieces which include attractive hand-painted cheese trays and handsome myrtlewood clocks.

Other items include myrtlewood incense, candles, perfume, necklaces, and some especially nice coasters.

Known mainly for its colorful and exotically grained wood, the wide-leaved myrtlewood tree blooms at Christmas time with small white blossoms; and in summer bears small fruit resembling olives. The large myrtlewoods in Oregon, estimated to be hundreds of years old, grow nowhere else in the world except for a much smaller variety found in the Holy Land.

Zumwalt's shop, started 25 years ago by the Zumwalt family, is now under new ownership, but the original owner still helps out behind the counter on occasion, showing myrtlewood gunstocks in basic styles and sizes which are handcrafted to individual guns on order, and cranberry candy in taffy or jelly squares—both specialties of the shop.

Zumwalt's guarantees all myrtlewood items sold and will pack and ship purchases anywhere in the United States. This is a good place to stop for those looking for the really different myrtlewood gift.

The Big Wheel is as close to an old-time general store as tourists are apt to encounter in a month of Sundays. It's cluttered, it's folksy, and visitors can find just about anything there if they look hard enough. Country clothes and cowboy boots crowd jewelry displays and rows of crocks. Jampacked racks of rain clothes hover over piles of deflated rubber boats. Displays of old-fashioned cards are tucked in among the souvenirs on the crowded countertops.

Up the plank stairs at the back, amid a jungle of plants, will be found (in season) incubators filled with cheeping fluffballs of new-hatched chicks and ducklings. Out on the old timbered dock, overalled clerks sling sacks of grain into waiting trucks in a setting that has all but disappeared since the advent of supermarkets. (Having a clerk call your pet food order from the checkout stand over a microphone to a boy in the storeroom, who rolls it out on a cart, isn't nearly as much fun as watching a husky young man hoist a bulging gunny sack of chicken feed by its ears and heave it over the tailgate into a pickup.)

Genial Charles Hettich doesn't miss a trick in promoting and maintaining the atmosphere of the old store which has been there since 1936, the year of the big fire which sent Bandon residents fleeing into the ocean to escape a flaming forest fire. Although he somehow gives the impression that he was hatched in one of his own incubators about the time the store was new, Hettich, a former electrical engineer on the East Coast, and his wife Lillian took over the Big Wheel a couple of years ago. He has a gift of gab that doesn't stop; and there is a lot of over-the-counter visiting going on most of the time. It is a right friendly place to do business, whether the buyer is a native or just passing through.

There's only one thing missing here—penny candy. But who knows? By the time this sees print there may even be an old glass-fronted case with shelves of sugar dots, Mary Janes, licorice whips, little wax milk bottles full of colored syrup; maybe even tiny tin pans of fudge complete with minuscule spoons. We can only hope...

Since it's just off the highway at 130 Baltimore Avenue, it's easy to check out on the way through Bandon. And Charles Hettich will go out of his way to make any visitors feel welcome whenever they drop in.

Andrea's Home Made Food is an experience not to be missed while in Bandon. The special recipes are prepared and served family style, according to the owner's choices for the day. Praise from peers is strong praise indeed. Andrea's comes highly recommended by the proprietress of the Plum Pudding in Brookings. No more need by said.

The Eat'n Station is clean, pleasant, and easy to spot on Highway 101. The menu features a variety of omelets, fruit pancakes with whipped cream, an oyster sandwich on toast; and the jam comes in glass pots instead of plastic boxes. Open 7 a.m. to 8 p.m. except Wednesdays, when they close at 4.

Number one choice for fine dining in Bandon is **The Bandon Boatworks** at the very end of the jetty road across from the old lighthouse. A warm, friendly atmosphere adds to the enjoyment of superb food served with fanfare. At the top-notch salad bar near the foot of the stairs leading to the upper level dining room, diners slice their own bread from fresh-baked loaves. In addition to specialties like Dover Sole (stuffed with shrimp, mushrooms, and Swiss cheese and baked in wine) and Chicken Mascote (chicken, artichoke, ham, mushrooms in cheese sauce), they also serve half-pound hamburgers. Reasonable prices for fine cuisine.

The West First Street Studio near Bandon's dock area has been converted to an indoor Japanese garden to display the works of Gary Ekker (pottery and ceramics) and Bernie Dalmazzo (bronze sculpture).

PORT ORFORD

Port Orford, the most westerly incorporated city in the continental United States, is a self-styled "working fishing village" of 1,100 people halfway between Bandon and Gold Beach. It is situated on the only natural deepwater harbor between San Francisco and Seattle.

The atmosphere is pleasantly relaxed here—a curious legacy for a community established after a bloody confrontation between a group of settlers and hostile Indians, who placed a one-hundred-year hex on the city after they were defeated by the intruders.

The colonists were men recruited in Portland, Oregon, in the spring of 1851 by merchant Captain William Tichenor, who planned to set up a trade station to supply the gold miners already operating in the region. Armed with handguns and a tiny cannon, the men were unloaded on a huge stone mound resembling a lumpy loaf of bread in the harbor. Cut off by the mainland at high tides, the rock offered the most defensible site along the beach where the unfriendly Indians were gathering to watch their landing.

Captain Tichenor planned to return within two weeks with supplies and reinforcements. The ship was barely out of the harbor before the Indians began harassment. The attack which followed was repulsed by the colonists but left some settlers wounded and several Indians dead.

The isolated white men managed to hold the Indians at bay for two weeks with promises to be gone at the end of that time. On the 15th day, with no relief ship in evidence, between three and four hundred Indians gathered on the beach and charged the rock a second time. Again the settlers held their own but, with ammunition running low, decided to make a run for it. They pretended to begin construction of a fort on the rock to draw attention of the Indians from their escape plans. When the Indians who were keeping watch over the intruders' activities left the rock unguarded to report the new developments to the warring chiefs, the embattled men escaped from the rock and went overland to the settlement on the Umpqua River to the north.

Three weeks overdue, Captain Tichenor finally landed 67 armed men at the site who built a blockhouse and established the present city.

In June, 1951, Port Orford staged a centennial celebration which also marked the end of the 100-year bad luck jinx that the Indians bestowed on the original settlement after the warring at Battle Rock.

And each Fourth of July, the Jetty Jubilee Celebration commemorates the city's dramatic founding with a re-enactment of the historic battle, fireworks, a parade, and the coronation of a senior citizen queen.

The Walking Tour

Highway 101 makes a wide right-angle turn as it comes through Port Orford and drops down to follow the ocean front. A walking tour centered around this corner includes a variety of interesting shops, identified by a symbolized seagull on the fronts.

The Wooden Nickel, on the right side of the highway coming from Bandon, has a large stock of myrtlewood tableware and small gift pieces in warm satiny finishes, with one end of the building given over to yarns and needle art supplies.

Right on 12th Street one block to Idaho is **Johnny's House of Wild Blackberries**. Owners Fran and Bruce Bruso offer homemade jams from organically grown Oregon berries in several flavors and will ship throughout the country (UPS) in lots of 12.

A block down (at Idaho and 11th) is **The Freestones**, where rockhounds can find tumblers, saws, other supplies, and rocks.

On the highway between 10th and 9th is located **Quarles Fine Arts Studio** which features oils of Oregon subjects— seascapes, landscapes, and portraits, including miniatures.

At **Humbug Studio** owners Brenda and Alan Mitchell have gathered an outstanding stock of unusual items. The small green shake studio is entered via a side walk sheltered closely by the wall of a neighboring building, where Brenda has painted an attractive mural opposite the sliding glass entry door.

Along with fine art and superior craft pieces, the Mitchells have included fun things. Just inside is one of the largest collections of hand-designed rubber art stamps on the coast: birds, animals, vehicles, flowers, trees—even an erupting volcano! An array of fanciful peel-off stickers in rainbow colors—butterflies, shells, dragons, unicorns and such—are sold by the yard.

They carry an impressive line of copper weathervanes. And displayed in one of the porthole windows at the front is a selection of art glass—fine painting in transparent glass enamel on hand-rolled clear glass. These original designs are executed by artisans at Glassmasters Studio in New York, duplicating techniques developed in the Middle Ages. Each piece is named and attributed to the designer artist, and comes with a 50-year guarantee against fading.

On the curve where the highway starts to dip downhill is **Knutson's Handcrafted Clocks**. Grandfather clocks of classic elegance, crafted by Lyle Knutson in myrtle, maple, black walnut, and other fine woods are bargains at four-figure prices.

The **Nature Park Deli and Natural Foods Store** on the corner of Oregon Street and Highway 101 specializes in natural Oregon products, in gift packs or off the shelves, including wines.

On the beach side of the highway, at Washington and 5th, is **Walter's Landing Leather**. The specialty here is custom leather goods. Since early 1974, when Howard and Jerry Walters opened their business, it has grown "year by year; month by month." Outstanding among the leather accessories manufactured here from scratch are sheepskin slippers, designed by the Walters, made from skins tanned with the wool left on to form a cuddly inch-thick lining. Hats made from sheepskin are designed in the same manner with the wool inside for warmth and comfort. Both hats and slippers are made entirely by hand and make unusual and practical gifts.

Nearby in the same block is the **Dive Shop**, with equipment and supplies for divers, both rental and for sale.

Across the street and down a tad is the **Pacific Folk and Fine Art Cooperative**, showroom for a group of 14 local artists whose works include drawings, paintings, photographs, jewelry, porcelain, and raku. Representative of the quality products on display here are those of Kirk Swiss, president of the group, and Molly Cooley, who does the publicity, a husband and wife team of potters. Under his **Earth and Fire Pottery** label, Kirk markets such innovative stoneware as double-wall planters made with an inner bowl built into an outer shell to form a reservoir. Ventilation cutouts in the surface give these a highly effective dimensional design. Molly's **Tidepool Pottery** label is found on functional table and cook wares that are lead free, dishwasher safe, ovenproof, and easily cleaned. Although they do not keep regular hours at their studio at 12th and Jackson, they welcome visitors.

A block up Jackson Street from the Co-op is the **Jolly Joy** shop where fresh and frozen fish is available, along with crab and salmon in season.

At the **Shell Shack** near the Battle Rock Wayside at the end of Jefferson Street are found novelties, ships, planters, and of course shells in variety.

On the docks at the end of 5th Street visitors can watch commercial fishing boats (from the fleet of 60 craft which operate here) unload at buying stations the year around; and when the seas are running high, get pictures of Port Orford's "fleet on wheels" being hoisted out of the harbor by large cranes.

Hungry walkers can enjoy a sandwich at **The Dock** near the dock area and purchase smoked salmon and fresh fish while they're there.

Or they can stop at **Madelaine's** back on the highway near the Wayside turnoff for homemade soups, fresh baked bread, home-style entrees (evenings), and pies (fresh strawberry recommended) that are out of this world! Open 11 a.m.-9 p.m., except Mondays and Tuesdays.

A great way to top off the tour is by stopping in at **The Peg**

Leg Saloon across the street from Madelaine's to enjoy the friendly atmosphere with games, music, beer, and free popcorn.

A visit to the **Prehistoric Gardens**, located midway between Port Orford and Gold Beach, offers a unique experience. The gardens, showing lifelike scale models of prehistoric animals in a natural rain forest setting, is one of the most unusual presentations of its kind in the world.

Developed by E.V. and Kari Nelson to scientific standards based on years of research, the replicas are posed among moss-draped trees hundreds of years old in thickets of ferns suggestive of jungle forests, and along banks of creeks and pools thick with outsized vegetation. One skunk cabbage found in the park had leaves measuring up to 7 feet in length.

Many visitors following the quiet paths among the natural dioramas bathed in a continally changing light show of sun and shadow are overwhelmed by a feeling of being lost in a segment of forgotten time. The exhibit is far more than a series of statues standing among the trees. The Nelsons have captured a sense of reality, in the way the models in an excellent wax museum seem "real." The creatures have been captured in "living" poses. One especially effective scene shows a pair examining a nest on the ground—one standing upright carefully cradling an egg, the other stooping to examine a broken shell. One somehow receives the impression of young parents returning to find their home has been violated.

After measuring skeletons in museums and studying the works of artist Charles R. Knight, famed for his paintings of prehistoric animals. Nelson constructed the models by shaping frames of steel and metal lath which were plastered with concrete and painted to complete the natural appearance. Technical advice was obtained from the Department of Anthropology at the University of Oregon. Over the years Nelson has collected an extensive paleontology library.

Unobtrusive plaques inserted in man-made stones give statistics and information relative to the exhibits. "The first tree-like plants 2 or 3 feet high evolved near the ocean's edge

Life-scale models of long-vanished creatures are posed among moss-draped trees hundreds of years old in the Prehistoric Gardens. The models are constructed of steel and concrete plaster after painstaking research through museums and other scientific sources. Plaques set into man-made rocks give basic information about the animals and the ancient environment in which they developed. This educational exhibit is one of the most fascinating along the Oregon coast and is located half-way between Port Orford and Gold Beach.

over 400 million years ago..." or "There are more than 10,000 species of ferns..." The creatures themselves are named and profiled briefly at each site.

The project was started in 1953 and is still evolving. A gift shop carries souvenir items which depict or relate to prehistoric animals. The Nelsons scout gift fairs on buying trips searching for worthwhile items. Dinosaurs, popular as mementos, are harder and harder to come by. Some replicas are still obtainable from Korea; some are hand-carved in Mexico from onyx; others are imported from Spain. But they are becoming scarce, and prices, as with almost everything else, have climbed steadily in the past few years. In desperation Nelson designed a baby dinosaur which is being used on gift items and souvenirs for sale. The shop was enlarged in 1978, and a museum is planned as a later addition.

E.V. Nelson, a self-described "forger and steeler" (he manufactured logging equipment for 20 years) has turned a lifelong interest in prehistoric creatures into an educational tourist attraction—one well worth exploring. A moderate charge keeps the Prehistoric Gardens within family vacation budgets.

Arizona Beach is one of the few resorts on the Oregon coast offering RV camping at the ocean's edge. The 200 sites along the beach in the privately owned campground allow RVers to step out of doors directly onto the sand. Spread at the base of coastal mountains, the park also has more sheltered spaces among the trees and meadows back from the shore.

But the sound of the surf will lull travelers to sleep from anywhere in the spacious resort, and the sea smell follows campers who explore the remnants of the old Stage Road near the location of the famous Arizona Beach Inn, an important stop on the stage route which linked California and Oregon coastal towns. The old Inn building burned in 1942, but the site is marked by a lovely shade tree which bears a plaque noting its historical background.

Arizona Beach Resort offers comprehensive facilities: in addition to RV spaces there are modern motel units, some with kitchens, plus an activity hall which is often reserved for family reunions. Tent spaces are also available.

Owners Clive and Carol Bullian operate a store and gift shop on the premises—a delightfully informal place of business which hosts a continuing checker tournament in one corner near a coffee pot which is seldom allowed to grow cold or empty.

Arizona Beach is one of the few resorts on the Oregon coast which accommodate recreational vehicles right at the ocean's edge. More than 200 RV spaces with electrical hookups for self-contained units are available bordering the beach, with full hookups located in the central portion of the resort park. The private beach is fine for swimming, beachcombing, surf fishing, and other similar activities. It is open the year around for groups and individuals.

All camp sites have electric hookups. Beach spaces, for obvious reasons, have no sewer hookups, but a dumping station on the grounds accommodates self-contained RVs. Gas and propane are for sale to campers.

This is a pleasant locale for a vacation stop, whether for a day or a week or an entire summer. The private beach affords swimming, surf fishing, driftwood and agate combing. A private road connects the main park with the beach by means of a highway underpass, a safety feature appreciated by parents. Nearby scenic mountain trails offer plenty of opportunity for hiking. And the Prehistoric Gardens are a short walk from the resort store.

Located midway between Port Orford and Gold Beach, Arizona Beach is one of the most popular campgrounds on the southern coast. During the four summer months visitors number well into the thousands. However, the resort is open the year around, and many groups take advantage of the less-crowded seasons for get-togethers. The Bullians recommend that reservations be made three months in advance during the summer season or on special holidays. But whenever guests come, they will enjoy a very special atmosphere in this resort.

And Just Down the Road...

The rustic setting of **Humbug Mountain Lodge**, seven miles south of Port Orford, makes it a fine family stop, whether for meals, browsing, or an overnight stay in the individual cabins scattered behind the main building. Fun for both adults and youngsters is the opportunity to catch trout in the stream near the lodge to be cooked and served to the lucky anglers later in the dining room.

Travelers can find groceries and gas, gifts and mementos at the resort. A special attraction is **Demori Designs**, which shows works of seven Northwest artists in a variety of mediums: jewelry, pottery, water colors, oils, and photography all are on display for viewing and sales at the gallery near the main lodge building.

The lodge is named for Humbug Mountain, which served the native Indians as a weather station before modern technology took over the task. According to legend, good weather is assured when the top of the 1,750-foot mountain is clear.

Low tide is the best time to seek out the elusive razor clams, most popular of the varieties found on the Oregon coast. Clammers must move fast to catch the razors which can disappear into the beach sand at the rate of 30 seconds/foot.

The most interesting exhibit in the Chetco Valley Museum in Brookings is an ancient iron mask, a casting of a woman's face. Discovered on Lone Ranch Beach in 1957, journalists speculate on the possibility that it may be a likeness of Britain's Queen Elizabeth, left near the site by Sir Francis Drake during his run along the northern coast nearly 400 years earlier.

Sea Explorers of the Oregon Coast

The Pacific Northwest Coast was one of the world's last major coastlines to be explored (barring the Arctic areas), and Oregon's was the end of the line. True, as early as the mid-16th century Spanish navigators had cautiously crept north from their bases in Latin America, but barely past the California border. Juan Cabrillo in 1542 reached a point to the north of San Francisco bay; and there is some indication that his pilot Ferrelo may have taken his small vessel a few degrees farther north—enough to have crossed the Oregon boundary latitude at 42 degrees—after Cabrillo's death put him in command. But if either man made a landing, it has not been noted in any known records.

Thirty-six years later Sir Francis Drake, the renowned buccaneer in the service of Queen Elizabeth at the advent of Great Britain's challenge to Spain for supremacy of the world's oceans, made a recorded landing on the California coast north of San Francisco. It's possible that he also made a brief landfall on the Oregon coast on the same voyage.

Stuffed to the gunwales with treasure from surprise raids on the Spaniard's Pacific ports, Drake's *Golden Hind*—100 tons capacity with a crew of 60—wallowed north along the California coastline to avoid retaliation from Spanish officials undoubtedly on the alert for the pirate ship's return by the southern route.

It's improbable that exploration was uppermost in Drake's mind at the time; not much was known of what lay to the north. But given his alternatives, he may have been taking a chance on finding the fabled Northwest Passage whose existence had been rumored since Magellan completed his circling of the globe in 1522. In any case, Drake is credited with naming the upper Pacific coastal area "New Albion," a designation which held for 200 years or more.

Records of Drake's voyage give conflicting coordinates for the northern point reached during his journey. By his own account dated June 3, 1578, the ship sailed into cold and fog which held for two weeks before he backtracked south to a small bay just north of San Francisco, making it impossible to chart course by either sun or stars. Estimates place his one northern landing between 43 and 48 degrees latitude, but either would be along the Oregon coast, and possibly the "bad bay" in which he was forced to seek shelter from the winds is located there.

His descriptions of extreme cold, barren shores, and snow-covered mountains read more like the Arctic than Oregon's "banana belt" south coast, but historians still speculate that the great explorer, knighted by Queen Elizabeth on his return from the three-year journey of conquest, may have landed somewhere in the vicinity of Cape Arago. And it was on the basis of his account of the trip up the Pacific coast that the English based future claims to ownership of the Oregon Country.

In 1602 Sebastian Viscaino, under orders from King Philip II of Spain, headed an expedition from Mexico to establish a colony in lower California. After discovery of the Bay of Monterey, a storm separated one of the three ships in the expedition. Viscaino went north to 42 degrees latitude and reported seeing "white bluffs" of a promontory which are generally considered to have been the present Cape Blanco.

Commander d'Aguilar of the separated frigate, believing Viscaino was still proceeding north when he had indeed turned south again, continued in that direction and logged the first written description of the Oregon coast at somewhere north of 43 degrees. It was d'Aguilar who gave the name of Blanco to the headland he described, but he also reported near it a river large enough to prevent the ship entering it for fresh water. There is no river near Cape Blanco (or Cape Orford as it was later named by Lt. Vancouver in 1792). And d'Aguilar thought the river which they could not enter might be the famous Strait of Anian, or the Northwest Passage, between the Atlantic and Pacific oceans. It is believed by some historians that the river he saw may have been the Umpqua to the north.

It was almost 175 years before another landing was made (perhaps) on the Oregon coast. In March, 1775, an expedition of two Spanish ships commanded by Bruno Heceta and Juan Francisco de Bodega y Quadra, on a voyage of exploration out of Mexico, landed somewhere north of Cape Mendocino, again possibly in Oregon. Storms swept them out to sea on leaving their sheltered bay, taking them north to the coast of Washington before another landing could be made.

On the return voyage down the coast on August 17, 1775, Heceta anchored off the mouth of the Columbia, at first believing it to be the legendary Strait of Juan de Fuca, not yet located although it had long been marked on existing maps. He logged his anchorage at 45 degrees and decided this could not be the strait supposedly found by a Greek ship's pilot Apostolos Valerianos (who used the name Juan de Fuca) while on a voyage of exploration in 1592, which was recorded as being between 47-48 degrees latitude. Although the titanic currents and blasting winds made it impossible for Heceta to enter the estuary, his description of the beaches, land conformations, and especially of Neahkahnie Mountain leave no doubt of his location.

Three years later on March 7, 1778, Captain James Cook, the English navigator, attempted a landing at Yaquina Bay. But storms kept him tacking along the coast looking for a harbor, and resulted in his naming Cape Foulweather below Depoe Bay for his frustrating experience, and Cape Perpetua for the Saint who had been martyred on that date 1600 years earlier.

Ultimately, he reached Nootka Bay on the west shore of Vancouver Island, having missed the mouth of the Columbia altogether. But before leaving the north seas, he sailed into the

Arctic Ocean until solid ice stopped his ship and dispelled once and for all the existence of the Northwest Passage connecting the world's two major oceans.

It was another 14 years before the American Captain Robert Gray finally found courage to take a ship over the bar through terrifying currents and crashing waves into the mighty river which, if not the Northwest Passage, served as one of the principal waterways for east-west traffic over the American continent before railroads tied the two coasts together with steel tracks.

And were it not for the capricious weather for which the Columbia River bar is famous (or infamous), it might today be known as Rio Heceta, after the Spanish name given the estuary for many years on the maps of Spain—Ensenada Heceta.

A driftwood shelter makes a snug harbor from the wind. Shelters are seen on most Oregon beaches which boast a collection of driftwood.

The rock formations along the Oregon coast north of Bandon are some of the most unusual in the world. The inverted cliffs lean out over crashing waves as if to fend off attacks from lashing tides which, over 40 million years, have carved them to their present shapes.

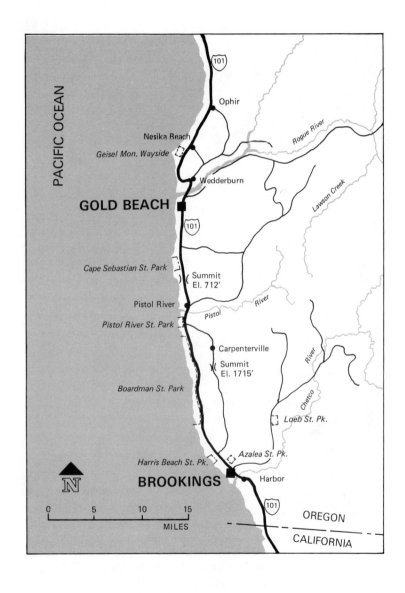

PACIFIC OCEAN

101

Ophir

Nesika Beach

Geisel Mon. Wayside

Rogue River

Wedderburn

Lawson Creek

GOLD BEACH

101

Cape Sebastian St. Park

Summit
El. 712'

Pistol River

Pistol River

Pistol River St. Park

Carpenterville

Summit
El. 1715'

River

Boardman St. Park

Chetco

Loeb St. Pk.

Azalea St. Pk.

Harris Beach St. Pk.

BROOKINGS

Harbor

N

| 0 | 5 | 10 | 15 |

MILES

101

OREGON

CALIFORNIA

Gold Beach
Brookings

GOLD BEACH

Gold Beach/Wedderburn bracket the mouth of the world-famous Rogue River, one of the nation's 10 "wild" waterways—Wedderburn on the north, Gold Beach on the south. Gold Beach is named for the gold found there by the miners who first settled the area. The community of Wedderburn was established by Robert D. Hume, who owned much of the land along the lower Rogue River at one time. Known as "the salmon king of the Rogue," Hume dominated the commercial salmon fishing in the area. When his cannery at Gold Beach was destroyed by fire, he floated the buildings which were saved across the river and set them up on the north bank of the river's mouth and continued his operations from the site of what is now the community of Wedderburn.

The Wild River

In early morning the Rogue, the focal point for the Gold Beach area, is hushed, mist-shrouded, as it nears its rendezvous with the Pacific. An hour later passengers will board the jet boats that will take them upriver 30 miles through an incomparable scenic wilderness; or carry them on another 20 miles into threshing white water and churning rapids channeled through narrow, rock-walled canyons. But for now the empty river craft move gently with the water's lapping. A seagull settles atop a piling to which one boat is tied and rests there; across the placid river mouth, cattle browse in an island meadow.

Soon enough the activity begins which will launch the morning trip. First down the skeletal ramp to the low floating docks is the dairyman carting boxes of milk—first of a series of delivery men who will load supplies for the isolated river lodges upstream.

Shortly after his appearance the passengers begin to desert the free coffee in the small booking office for the mini-decks that overlook the boats. They all wear jackets (the morning is cool) and hats (protection against a later sunburn). Most carry cameras and sunglasses.

A few minutes before the 8:30 departure time, the pilots, professional guides and boatmen, come down the ramp and wait to assist the passengers who follow into the open boat. When all are seated comfortably, the engines thrust to life, the boat makes a sweeping curve into the current, and the trip has begun.

The ride to Agness, terminal of the half-day trips, is a leisurely scenic journey through country which gradually makes the transformation from coastal environment to river wilderness. Traveling by boat affords a different perspective than is gained from the hill road which curves and winds along the rim of the cliffs bordering the river. Along the lower Rogue the green of fir and cedar, oak and madrona are soft-ened by the paler greens of wild shrubs. In spring fuchsia and azaleas gleam in Easter-egg pinks and oranges among the green; wild iris and ceanothus make "dilly-dilly" patches of lavender-blue, highlighted by the sun-yellow of buttercup and mustard. In September the fiery reds of Indian paintbrush and patimous burn boldly on the hillsides.

A camera is a must on the river trips up the Rogue. Where else could a photographer have a ringside seat to "shoot" a half dozen fresh-water otter sharing a dinner of just-caught salmon on a river rock? Boat pilots pull inshore and

The last passengers are helped aboard the boat, eager to begin the six-hour trip up the scenic Rogue River, which will include a leisurely lunch at world-famous Lucas Lodge, a landmark on the Rogue for over 75 years.

stop frequently for such sideshows, giving passengers close-ups of deer, bear, coyotes, and sometimes wild pig; plus beaver, racoon, and once in awhile, elk. The river is a paradise for bird lovers also, harboring osprey, golden eagles, blue heron, and snowy egrets among the countless varieties of bird life along its shores.

Historical landmarks too are seen along the way: sites of Indian confrontations during the years of unrest among the Rogues; crumbling artifacts abandoned by miners who were the Rogue's first settlers. The pilots, well versed in local lore, are glad to answer questions.

High spot of the trip may well be lunch at historic Lucas Ranch at Agness, the old farmhouse turned lodge where, for over 75 years, the Lucas family has been serving home-cooked meals from their own garden products to river travelers. Founded by Larry Lucas, long-time unofficial "Mayor of the Rogue," it is now operated by his son Willard, who has tried hard to keep it unchanged. The food is served family style in the long glassed-in dining room where tables and benches are covered in red bandana-patterned oil cloth. Old kerosene lanterns and lamps hang from the ceiling beams, until recent years the only lighting for evening dining.

A typical summer menu will feature fried chicken and Swiss steak; fresh corn on the cob, sliced tomatoes, and potatoes from the ranch garden on the slope above the house; with ice cream and fresh raspberries for dessert.

It is not unusual for the lodge to feed up to 150 guests at a sitting. And it's safe to say the fame of Lucas' home-grown, home-cooked meals have spread around the globe by word of mouth through famed personages who, like President Herbert Hoover, have fished and boated the Rogue. Many, having experienced the beauty of the region, have become residents; among them western writer Zane Gray and, more recently, the lovely film star Ginger Rogers.

There is time at the noon stop for passengers to relax in the outdoor courtyard ringed by great shade trees and "furnished" with tables made of thick slices of native logs. To one side a grapevine 90-plus years old roofs a room-sized trellis. They'll have time, too, to pick up incidentals or mementos at the small store in the front of the lodge. Some may even want to explore the Agness "airport"—a landing strip centering a pasture beyond the Lucas vegetable garden, which may require pilots to chase grazing cattle off the runway before takeoff.

If Lucas Ranch is the granddaddy of Rogue resorts, **Singing Springs**, alternate meal stop at Agness for the jet trips, is a most attractive young adult in its twenties. Singing Springs Ranch offers modern guest cottages with private baths and view windows—even porches—mid-April to mid-November.

Owners Rudy and Delores Valenta feature home-cooked meals served outdoors "with a smile" to boat passengers, who may also enjoy wine and beer in the charming patio shaded by old myrtlewood and fir trees. Passengers will have time here to look around the naturally landscaped ranch gardens, or to browse the distinctive gift shop.

The boat, which also carries mail to the upriver communities, pulls away from its mooring and heads into the sweeping curve that will take the boat around the island and into its course for a trip the passengers will never forget. ˙

Both morning and afternoon trips, six hours long, are
made to Agness, terminal point of the original mail boat run
which began in 1895 to provide postal service to settlers who
were inaccessible by roads. An all-day trip carries passengers 20 miles farther upriver into rocky channels boiling with
white water, as far as Paradise Canyon where rock cliffs
loom 1,500 feet above the river's surface. Boats making the
trip beyond Agness, where the "truly wild river" begins, are
small, designed to challenge the unruly Rogue on its own
terms, piloted by licensed guides who know the upper river
well.

For all the rugged, untamed beauty of the Rogue, the
river trips are sage and comfortable. All jet craft making the
runs are manufactured at Gold Beach to rigid Coast Guard
standards. They vary in size from 10 to 35 passenger capacity. Pilots on all river boats must pass Coast Guard examina-
tions before being certified.

Companies operating the Rogue River jet boat trips are
both located at the mouth of the river: **Jerry's Rogue River Jet
Boats** on the south side of the bridge in Gold Beach; **Courts
White Water Trips**; **Rogue River Mail Boat Trips** (pioneer mail
service begun in 1895, with passenger service since the
1930's) both on the north side of the river at Wedderburn.

Reservations are not required, but are advisable, for boat
trips and for lunch or dinner at the upriver resorts, especially
during the summer season.

Tu Tu Tun Vacation Lodge seven miles upriver on the
north bank of the Rogue is one of the finest on the coast.
Fishing for the world-famous Chinook salmon and steelhead
is one of the main attractions offered by this superior resort,
but it is only one of the many features that make it unique.

The rustic modern buildings overlooking the river house
a central lobby which boasts a wall-sized rock fireplace, a
cozy lodge, and a dining room which features round tables
(comfortable for six) with lazy susan turntables for convenient home-style serving. The menu offers fresh meats,
seafood, and vegetables and fruits, and there are always
snacks at hand between times. Breakfast is served early for

those who are eager to get out on the river, and packed lunches will be prepared on order. To top it off, an angler's catch can be the entree for the evening meal if desired.

Rooms are beautifully appointed to reflect the exclusive but casual atmosphere, and each has a private balcony with a river view, plus special racks for fishing equipment and outdoor gear. Drying rooms are there for taking care of wet clothing.

Guests not interested in fishing will find plenty of recreational activity to help them enjoy a perfect stay. A pitch and putt course, horseshoes, and a heated swimming pool are part of the lodge facilities along with a recreation room with an antique pool table and a player piano. Outdoor activities also include horseback riding, a golf course nearby, hiking, excursion boat trips upriver on the jet boats which stop daily at the private dock to pick up guests for the scenic boat trips. Sightseeing flights are available from **Pacific Air Services** operating out of the Gold Beach Airport where both charter and private flights can use the landing strip. Transportation to and from the airport is furnished by the lodge.

Fishermen must bring their own gear, but licenses are obtainable at Tu Tu Tun. For those bringing their own boats, arrangements can be made through the lodge for fishing guides as well as for anglers who wish to hire them. Lodge personnel will also care for the catch and hold it until departure, either fresh or frozen for shipping.

The service at Tu Tu Tun is on the American plan, and rates include three meals a day in addition to lodging. For a vacation which combines exclusive comfort with accessibility to coastal activities, Tu Tu Tun is almost unbeatable.

Some Shops to Explore

The Gull Gallery on Highway 101 north of Gold Beach expresses the discriminating tastes of its owners Stan and Marie Foster, not only in the quality gifts they carry but in the decor of the shop itself. From the outside The Gull Gallery resembles many others along the coast. But the interior is another story. Stan Foster has used an imaginative approach to make use of coastal materials in unusual ways.

A display wall of random length driftwood shakes provides the perfect background for sand-polished driftwood carvings of coast birds and marine life. Thick ceiling beams of driftwood from an old cannery offer a perfect drop for hangings.

A tone of quality is emphasized throughout the gallery. The scrimshaw chests are exquisite; shells seem special somehow; paintings and drawings hold the interest of the browser from wall to wall.

Prints by writer-photographer Ione Reed, uniquely mounted on weathered driftwood panels, are something different in coast art. Dainty shell pins by one local craftswoman 76 years young resemble miniature valentines.

Visitors who take advantage of the Fosters' offer to "Let The Gull do your beachcombing for you!" will be in excellent hands.

The **Pelican's Pouch** contains just about everything the gift buyer could want in the arts/crafts line: jewelry, myrtlewood, pottery, stained glass, paintings, carvings—they're all to be found at one convenient location. The gallery is easy to spot as the traveler enters Gold Beach.

By the Rogues, on the highway just down from The Gull Gallery, features handcrafted jewelry and ceramics by partners Fran Putnam and Jo Bailey. They also offer ongoing weekly classes in ceramics, with more structured classes in silversmithing. The shop carries some fine imported gifts (framed exampes of fine European needlework are especially attractive) as well as works of local crafts artists (hand-executed belt buckles, for instance).

An alcove serves as a showroom for **The Bionic Chair**—one piece, shaped back and seat, without legs, which rocks on the floor, upholstered in velour with matching drum-shaped footstools. These are good news for floor sitters, who will have to try them to believe how comfortable they are.

Don't miss **The Glass Apple**, a nearby shop that specializes in fragile things: stained glass of all kinds, lamps, studio windows; plus tools and classes for do-it-yourselfers.

The Beach Mall across from the courthouse on Highway 101 houses several businesses, including **Beautee Land Beauty Salon**, and **Tree-Anon**, an attractive women's fashion shop.

And then there's the **Sugar Shoppe**, the chocoholics' dream of a candy store. Along with the large selection of candies one expects to find in such places, this one offers some delightful novelty items. For instance: solid chocolate greeting cards, about 4 × 6 inches BIG, with appropriate messages—Happy Birthday or Be My Valentine—surrounded by molded flowers and scrolls. They are thin enough to look like the real things (maybe a quarter of an inch) and thick enough to satisfy the appetite of a true chocolate addict.

Frank Paucker, a retired technician with Disney enterprises, makes his own soft-center chocolates, 32 flavors, with whipped cream filling, in light and dark coatings. He also has dreamed up an inviting natural fruit bar which is one of the best sugarless confections you'll find anywhere. Dates, figs, seeds, nuts, and honey go into this tasty candy.

You can pick up fine coffees and teas here. And jars of penny candy are placed on low shelves for young customers who like to ponder the choices before blowing their allowances on goodies.

Paucker says he'll ship candies anywhere if postage is included with orders, except during hot weather.

Pleasant Places to Eat

Grant's is a breakfast and lunch place (6 a.m.-4 p.m.) offering 35 omelets ranging in price from $2.65-$5.10 (the latter a fisherman's omelet filled with crab, shrimp, or salmon). Several kinds of pancakes and waffles are listed. All regular breakfasts are served with grits if desired. Best news of all: coffee is 15¢ with meals; otherwise 30¢. An assortment of sandwiches listed includes avocado with bacon and a Spanish burger, both good. Grant's is located a short distance off the highway on the south side of the river, next door to Indian Creek Campground (take the first turn left as you come off the bridge from the north).

The Captain's Table at the south end of Gold Beach on Highway 101 is recommended. An interesting decor makes for a pleasant atmosphere; the food is excellent. Try this one.

The Golden Egg serves breakfast all day. From 6 a.m. to 9 p.m. seven days a week they prepare an assortment of exotic omelets on order. The Golden Egg is easy to find on South Ellensburg Street (Highway 101).

The Sportsman's Grotto caters to fishermen, but their menu is comprehensive. The Grotto, on the north side of the river just off the Highway and their **Porterhouse Room** in Gold Beach proper serve all kinds of foods to tempt the hungry sportsman, from the Seafarer Omelet (crab, shrimp, scallops, clams, onion, and mushrooms) to southern fried chicken. And if you have a companion along, The Affectionate Omelet (for two) is a dilly. Best of all, they stay open around the clock; dinner is served at both restaurants beginning at 4 p.m.

Riley's On The Rogue, noted for the fine seafood and steaks served in the restaurant, also offers motel accommodations and facilities for trailers, plus a dock and tackle shop. The dining room is open 5 to 10 p.m. Riley's is located a mile off Highway 101 on the South Bank Road.

Jot's Resort on the north bank of the river offers rooms, restaurant, and lounge, plus boat rentals and a sports shop. Court's White Water Trips jet boats depart from their docks for the daily run up the Rogue.

Some Special Parking Places

Chuck and Gerry Knox, operators of **Indian Creek Recreation Park** may not be able to offer everything to make campers happy, but they sure give it a good try. From the moment an RVer turns into the attractive grounds overlooking the mouth of the Rogue River, he'll feel welcome.

Many of the 100 hookups for RVs are clustered around central shelters which offer the perfect set-up for family reunions or ground camping. And there is a special section for tenters among the natural wooded areas at the back of the park.

Vacationers could spend weeks at Indian Creek without leaving the grounds if they were a mind to. The laundry, store (groceries and gifts), and Pancake House are just a stroll away from the hookup sites. In the lodge building is an upstairs recreation room with pool tables, a piano, television, and games of all kinds. There are outside activity areas for both children and adults, too. Both the recreation room and the outdoor barbeque can be reserved for private parties.

But it is the little extras that make this park special. The park office personnel will give guests information on all restaurants in the vicinity, including copies of their menus; will help guests find a baby sitter, or point them in the direction of a beauty shop. They have an activity list of things to do in the Gold Beach area and will even make reservations for guests if they are required. Best of all, prices are most reasonable in spite of the special attention they give their patrons.

It's a good place to settle in for a night or a week, or even longer. Indian Creek Park is easy to find a half mile from the highway on the south bank of the Rogue.

Sandy Camp on Ocean Side Drive in Gold Beach offers attractive accommodations for RVers from May through October. Available are 35 modern pull-through hookups and 50 self-contained spaces with hot showers, restrooms, and garbage service. There is no extra charge for cars or pets. Prices are computed on a basic charge per vehicle and persons, but they are leveled off at a maximum charge per party, which is most reasonable. Bait and tackle and ice are also available here at this camp near the beaches. Office hours are 8 a.m. to 9 p.m. for visitors' convenience.

The Pioneer

If the *Mary D. Hume* had been a human instead of a schooner, she would have become a soldier of fortune. A native Oregonian, she derived from good pioneer stock. Her birthplace was a small cove near Mill Rock at the south end of the bridge over the Rogue at Gold Beach. Her ancestors knew no peers. Her keel, $10' \times 36' \times 140'$ was hand-squared from a majestic Douglas fir and floated down the Rogue from Lobster Creek to the building site. But like many a frontier lady she began life using some "pre-tested" accoutrements: her engine was a hand-me-down from an older sister-ship which came to a bad end at an early age, wrecked after a single trip to San Francisco.

The *Mary D.* made her own way to San Francisco in February of 1881, but during her early years made most of her calls in smaller "dog hole" ports delivering materials loaded out of the glamorous California harbor. And when, after eight years of freight runs along the northern coast, the Pacific Steam Whaling Company bought her for duty in the far North, the *Mary D. Hume*, smallest ship in the company fleet, moved into her new role with zest.

Refitted and refurbished to handle a cargo of whalebone, she headed for the Arctic, there to spend 29 months—one of the first whalers to be ice-locked into a winter-long station. And like many a lady who sought her fortunes in the frozen North, she came home with a treasure valued at $400,000, the most lucrative cargo in the history of American whaling.

Details of her career following her whaling days are sketchy, but what facts do emerge indicate the feisty adventuress was not subdued after retiring as a star of the whaling fleet to resume a lesser role as a commercial tug between Puget Sound and Alaska. In 1904 she was sunk by ice in the Nushgak River which empties into Alaska's Bristol Bay, but was rescued and taken to Seattle for repairs; later turning up as a halibut fishing boat for a brief unprofitable venture before returning to tugging and log-raft towing.

But, as it will, time overtook the gallant lady as she went into her nineties, and the *Mary D.*, which once had been known for her triumphant *firsts* began to be noticed for her *lasts*.

She was among the few tugs who still sounded bells on Puget Sound when the ships bells were silenced by changes in maritime procedures in 1970. At the time of her retirement by the American Tugboat Company in 1977, the *Mary*

D. was the oldest commercial tug still working on the West Coast, and the last survivor of the American fleet of Arctic steam whalers.

Still, hers was not to be the fate of many a footloose lady forced to live out her declining years as a stranger in a strange land. Crowley Maritime Corporation, owner of the *Mary D. Hume,* made sure the grand old lady of the Northwest coastal waters would spend her remaining days among loved ones in the country of her origin by presenting her to the Curry County Historical Society and the Port of Gold Beach.

On August 31, 1979, at high tide near high noon, the *Mary D. Hume,* escorted by two 44-foot Coast Guard boats and a minor parade of small craft, returned to the Rogue River as hundreds of spectators lined the jetties to applaud her final entry into her home port.

The *Mary D. Hume* rests there now, and visitors can see her rocking gently in her berth within sight of her birthplace—the land originally owned by Robert D. Hume, Rogue River's salmon king, who christened her a hundred years ago as the namesake of his wife, Mary Duncan Hume.

BROOKINGS

Brookings, just seven miles north of the California border, is the coastal gateway city for Oregon. Brookings Harbor, one of the safest on the coast, is a fascinating place to be in the late afternoon when the fishing boats return from their day's travel to the modern facilities. The harbor offers berths to both sport craft and the 150 commercial fishing boats which moor there.

Nearby **Sporthaven** park is one of the few places along the coast where RVers can step out of the mobile "homes away from home" and be within spitting distance of the ocean. Located on the sandy spit which banks the Brookings boat basin from the ocean, Sporthaven is a perfect spot for those who come to fish, and a fun stopover for travelers who want an interesting place to tie down overnight.

The jetty provides a natural grandstand for watching the boats come trundling into harbor as the day begins to fade and makes an ideal perch for land anglers. Photographers find the basin a delight, with small craft assuming Easter-egg colors as they come into the basin and line up along the docks near the tall-masted sailing vessels.

Fish cleaning stations, ice, gas, and picnicking facilities are also found here.

At the very end of the spit is the **Chetco River Coast Guard Station**. Near the buildings is a small memorial to the 10 Coast Guard crewmen who were lost in a storm on August 16, 1972, especially honoring the two who were never found.

Also located on the Lower Harbor Road is the **Driftwood Travel Trailer Retreat**. The name is well given. The RVers stopping here are sheltered by shade trees while still being within easy access of the beach. The all-electric hookup and drive-through spaces are quiet and secluded; a laundry and a recreation room are convenient.

Owners Walt and Iva Thompson offer an additional attraction to the fishing and beach activities for those who wish to spend longer periods of time in their pleasant park-like surroundings: free classes in driftwood art. Needed craft supplies can be purchased through them.

Over on Highway 101 the **Chetco Travel Trailer Resort** a mile south of the Chetco Bridge offers over 100 drive-through spaces and 96 hookups, plus adult recreation facilities and a laundry. And they welcome overnighters.

Some Interesting Places to See

A couple of miles south of the Chetco River Bridge an older red-and-white house overlooks Highway 101 from a pastoral hill setting. This is the **Chetco Valley Historical Society Museum** and well deserves time spent exploring the artifacts it harbors.

The house itself was serving as a stagecoach way station and trading post before Abraham Lincoln became president, owned and operated by pioneer law officer Harrison Blake.

The building is filled now with furnishings and tools and

In late afternoon the fishing fleet returns to Brookings Harbor, one of the safest on the Oregon coast. The boat basin is home to 150 commercial fishing boats and offers mooring for a large number of sport and recreational boats. In early morning when they parade out to sea and in the evening when they return, the jetty is a favorite observation point for vacationers from the nearby campgrounds.

mementos of pioneer times similar to those found in small museums everywhere: a spinning wheel, old sewing machines, a small trunk made in 1706 brought around Cape Horn; plus a collection of Indian relics—baskets and arrowheads and an ancient dugout canoe.

There are even some Japanese swords, recalling the area's claim to being the only spot on the United States mainland to come under aerial attack during World War II. On September 9, 1942, a Japanese plane dropped fire bombs a few miles east of Brookings with minimal damage, although it was judged at the time to have been a retaliation raid for General Doolittle's raid on Tokyo.

By far the most exciting exhibit, however, is an iron casting of a woman's face, fragile and flaking from years of exposure to sand and sea. At least one Northwest author has made a plausible case for its being a relic left by Sir Francis Drake at his still unidentified landfall on the North Pacific Coast during his journeys of 1579. On June 10, 1979, the 400th anniversary of the first recorded sighting of the Oregon coast at Cape Arago, and possible landing of the great explorer in a small cove to the north, were commemorated by appropriate ceremonies conducted by members of the Oregon Historical Society at the site.

The mask, discovered on Lone Ranch Beach in 1957, might well be an image of Drake's patroness Queen Elizabeth of England. Certainly it depicts a woman of a century long gone, and certainly it is far older than the earliest colonists' arrival at this place on the Northwest Coast.

The museum is open on winter weekends from 9 a.m. to 5 p.m., Friday through Sunday; on summer afternoons from noon until 5 p.m. But the attendant lives nearby and has, upon occasion, obliged visitors by opening the museum during off hours.

On the hill near the short flight of stairs which lead up from the highway grows the National Champion Cypress Tree, verified as the world's largest. The tree—99 feet tall with a spread of over 100 feet and a trunk more than 27 feet in circumference—shelters a pair of resident owls who have lived there for years.

The grounds surrounding the museum, part of the Pedri-olli Brothers Ranch until the house was donated to the Historical Society in 1970, offers an opportunity to stretch legs while returning for an hour or so to an earlier, more romantic, and probably less hectic era; as interesting to adults as to children.

One of the most tranquil spots on the southern Oregon coast is **Azalea State Park** just outside the city limits of Brookings. This beautiful hillside setting where the main events of the annual Memorial Day weekend Azalea Festival are held stands out as an oasis of loveliness in an area where natural beauty is routine.

The park is literally filled with azaleas of all sizes, from low borders to tree-shrubs 20 feet or more in height. Some are over 300 years old. The azaleas bloom from April through June, but even when the blossoms are not splashing pastel free-form designs against the background of shiny green foliage, the shrubs and trees and paths and glens of the park afford a pleasant place for a picnic.

Sheltered spaces are centered with tables of myrtlewood made of planks 4 inches thick, the grainings and color shadings highlighted by layers of protective coating. Built by members of the Civilian Conservation Corps during the 1930's, each table required half a dozen men to set it into place. A covered shelter has electric stoves and sinks for those who favor a cookout. A stone gazebo at one high spot invites strollers to rest and view the breathtaking spectacle of acres of delicate blooms in late spring.

A natural amphitheater banked by gentle slopes has a stage from which the Azalea Festival Queen and her court are presented. The annual parade, drawing thousands of spectators and hundreds of participants, also ends here.

The festival weekend is filled with events and exhibits to keep visitors in a festive frame of mind. The problem for many may be to find time to take in everything. There are art shows and flower shows; a book sale and a flea market; an old-time fiddlers contest, square dancing, and a waterball tournament; an Air Festival and a Hill Climb; a community church service on Sunday and a Memorial Service on Monday during which wreaths are cast into the harbor in memory of those lost at sea. Purchase of a weekend ticket covers a seafood luncheon and a beef barbecue—both held at the park.

Azalea State Park provides a fitting background for this celebration, memorable among coast events for over 40 years. A well-marked exit from Highway 101 at the south end of Brookings takes visitors onto Park Road and to the entrance of the park.

Eight miles up the Northbank Road along the Chetco River is **Loeb State Park** with picnic facilities among a large grove of myrtlewood trees. Loeb Park encompasses one of the finest stands of this beautiful evergreen tree, which grows only in Coos and Curry Counties in Oregon, and in Palestine in the Holy Land. A redwood grove adjoins the myrtlewoods. Loeb Park is far enough inland to enjoy sunshine even on the foggiest days, and there is excellent swimming and fishing here also.

The Lilies of the Field

Oregon's Curry County at the southwestern corner of the state, together with neighboring Del Norte County in California, produces over 90 percent of the Easter lilies grown in the United States. This million dollar industry began to flourish with the advent of World War II when the bulbs were no longer available from Japan.

Daffodils too are a major crop here; and other nursery specialties include hydrangeas and geraniums as well as commercial versions of the azaleas and rhododendrons which cover the coastal slopes with color during the spring.

Strahm's Lilies at Harbor just south of Brookings is representative of the commercial lily farms in the area. Ruth and Harve Strahm have been growing lilies for over 20 years. The bulbs, which bloom late May through August, are harvested in September. During the winter months— November through March—they are busy packing and mailing orders all over the United States and to many foreign countries. Their bulbs find their way to France, Germany, Canada; they even ship bulbs to Holland. And they receive requests from the Soviet Union now and then.

What sets the Strahms apart is that they specialize in pink lilies—from palest blush to deep fiery red. Many of the names in their catalogue of oriental lilies reflect this emphasis: Pink Bouquet, Blushing Bell, Ruby Jewel strain, Red Dragon, Coralbee, Firebrand, Red Jamboree—

Recently developed are the true deep-red varieties which are just coming into their own. Other colors included in the more than 60 varieties listed in their brochures are white, yellow, gold (shading to browns), and countless combinations of these tones. It's safe to say shoppers can find almost any color lily at the Strahm farm—except blue. To date they have not been able to develop or find a true blue lily. But they keep looking, because customers keep asking for one.

The Strahms are friendly and gracious, and welcome visitors to the bulb farm, especially when the acres of blooms spread color over the fields. Even for the casual gardener, the tour is a fascinating experience. Lilies range in size from a foot high to almost 12 feet tall, with blooms from 6 to 12 inches across. The Strahms dispense information on the care and cultivation of lily bulbs, personally and in the literature they have available.

The **Pink Lily Farm** is easy to find by turning off Highway 101 one mile south of the Chetco Bridge on Benham Lane which curves south onto Oceanview Drive. Once headed in the right direction, signs direct visitors right to the greenhouses, a short drive through a rural area in which flowers flourish.

Some Out-of-the-Ordinary Shops

If there is one shop in Brookings which must not be overlooked, **Tina's By The Sea** is the one. For here are found the "knothead" wood carvings—fantastically detailed heads whose faces reveal such character viewers must keep reminding themselves these are not living beings.

Members of a generation which has embraced Will Huygen's "Gnomes" with open arms will lose their hearts on sight to these "people" (it is almost impossible to think of them as statues or sculptures) developed from wood knots which have been tossed and tumbled on the ocean's currents for enough years to erode a log to the irreducible core of burled growth.

Polished by the seas' churnings, the knots emerge smoothed but grained, the soft wood long since disappeared, the bole revealing an uncanny resemblance to lined and wrinkled faces of humans who have emerged from life's storms, scarred but invincible.

It is difficult to focus on any one of these remarkable carvings as outstanding. Each is a masterpiece in its own right, the features and characters indicated by the knot's formation. Artist Tina Foster heightens the human likeness by carving and reshaping, using dental tools for the fine detail work; then painting lifelike color into faces and clothing. The combination of natural wood "skin"—whether smooth or grained—and eyes of a soft blue or hazy green or snapping black is amazingly realistic.

The conformation of the knots seems to lend them to transformation into pirates and gnomes and oriental sages. One pirate dominated the display wall, seeming almost life-size (although he wasn't) and ready to come stumbling across the shop to demand tribute from patrons shopping there.

The star of the show, however, was an Old Man of the Sea looking as if he had materialized full-grown on the shore to manipulate his nets and lines.

There are other expressive examples of coastal art in the shop. Tina's mother and father, both retired in the early 1970's, continue to create driftwoodoramas, weavings, and hangings which approach the status of fine art. Old wooden pulleys mounted on weathered driftwood are just one example of their creative works.

Bookends, coral, jewelry, sea animals, shells, and ships—all of these are found here. But it will be the knotheads (originated by Tina, imitated not-quite-convincingly by other artists in other shops) which will hold visitors enthralled.

Tina's By The Sea is located at the north end of Brookings on the Highway.

The Central Building

A group of small shops quartered in the Central Building will be of interest to travelers. The building is old, refurbished to resemble a colonial mansion. Painted white with black iron accents, it is easy to spot on Highway 101 at the south end of town just before crossing the bridge to the Harbor district.

Nan-El's Treasure Trove features quality gifts and coastal art and crafts, coral paintings, some exotic sea shells, soft sculptures in variety; plus wines and gift food specialties.

The Breeze Bookstore carries maps, posters, and a large stock of books about the Oregon Coast. Prints and photographs by local artists are displayed here also.

All major publishers are represented in the stock here, and they give careful attention to special orders.

Across the street from Central Building is **Yesteryears**, which deals in jewelry, glass, art glass, primitives, plus American and European antique furniture. It's the kind of nonspecialist shop that is fun to poke around in whether or not the client is in the mood for buying. The landmark feature of Yesteryears is its free-hanging sign of stained glass designed by local glass artist Patricia Cate.

Just down the block the **Basement Boutique** attracts passersby with a display window framed in worm-eaten barn boards decorated with heavy rope. Owner Jeannette Stevenson offers a unique combination of imports and local arts/crafts.

A fine collection of soft ware is found here—dolls and pillows and toys which are different. For instance, Jeannette's Wall Worm, a 36×8 inches green cloth "worm" hung lengthwise from curtain rings, with pockets for storing toys, crayons, and other small treasures.

An unusual line of playthings are Vegemals from Freemountain Toys, which includes a carrot, an ear of corn, a sprig of broccoli all 24 inches tall; and a peanut pillow that zips open to reveal two small peanut-shaped cloth balls. Among animals in the collections is a "birthing cow"—a black and white Holstein type which does, indeed, carry a small stuffed calf in its interior.

Outstanding among the many fine gift items are mirrors framed behind hand-carved wood silhouette frames.

The Brookings Harbor Shopping Center across the Chetco River in Harbor is a good one-stop rest for leg-stretching and picking up those items and services all vacationers need sooner or later. Beginning with a post office, shoppers will find a coffee shop, a barber and beauty shop, laundromat, drugstore, novelty shops, hardware store, department store, and a bakery.

Driftwood Craft House near the shopping center shows crafts from driftwood and other natural materials, and offers demonstrations on creative craftwork.

For leatherworkers or those interested in leather gifts, **The Crafted Cow** two and a half miles south of the Chetco Bridge has just about everything in the leather line. In addition to leather clothing they have accessories, sandals, and moccasins. Owners Bill and Becky Thompson also have all hardware and craft materials for leathercrafters who work up their own ideas. And they repair shoes, saddles, purses, boots—even zippers.

Beautiful You in the Tower Mall at Brookings Harbor Shopping Center specializes in natural ingredient cosmetics with an emphasis on Aloe Vera products. Owner Marilee Willson offers services customers seldom find these days. A free facial is given for the asking; she also gives demonstrations and advice on nail care. Fine beauty products, packaged under the Beautiful You label, are priced 30%-50% lower than comparable brands, and 1980 prices are guaranteed in effect throughout 1981. Good news for vacationers: she fills mail and phone orders anywhere in the country.

Accessories here are in the "something special" category. Designer sunglasses by Jacques Martain of Paris featuring precision-ground plastic lenses in unique frames are priced from $6-$18.

Handbags ranging in price from $10-$60 are all manufactured in Oregon, including canvas bags made to Marilee's design. True bargains can be found here in fine rolled-gold jewelry, and crystal earrings imported from Austria. Hours are from 10 a.m.-5:30 p.m., Monday through Saturday.

Morey's Arts is a gallery showing the paintings of Peggy Morey, a former teacher whose paintings are shown in collections around the country. The other half of the family team is Ralph, who handles the custom framing operation operated in connection with the gallery. They also carry a complete line of art supplies for vacationers and local artists. On Highway 101, downtown.

Some Thoughts For Food

Flying Gull Restaurant adjacent to the Brookings Inn at the north end of Brookings is open from 6 in the morning to 10 at night daily and features seafood on their extensive menu. This is a friendly place for lunch or dinner.

Jo-Lo's on the highway coming into town is open every day 5 a.m.-7 p.m.; goodies here include homemade pastry and sack lunches.

The Coast House is that "someplace special" for dining out in Brookings. They feature steaks, seafood, and a large wine list. Lunches weekdays 11 a.m.-3 p.m.; dinners daily.

Visitors to Brookings by-pass **The Plum Pudding** to their sorrow. Now located in the Central Building, Highway 101 downtown, their menu features Russian-Jewish dishes of superb quality. A specialty of the day is offered, plus unusual sandwiches on a choice of homemade breads. And the dessert list is enough to make anyone, anywhere, renounce the dieting forever. The clincher is the bread basket, a coffee break idea that can't be topped: an assortment of bread samples in a small basket to accompany that rarity of rarities, a mug of good hot full-bodied coffee.

EVENTS CALENDAR

February

Seaside—Beachcomber's Festival—Middle
Tillamook—Swiss Mid-Winter Festival—Middle
Seaside—Trail's End Marathon—Late
Newport—Seafood & Wine Festival—Late

March

Newport—Blessing of the Fleet—Early
Tillamook—Trask River Raft Races—Early
Brookings—Beachcomber & Driftwood Festival—Middle
Yachats—Arts & Crafts Fair—Middle
Nehalem—Canoe Races—Late

April

Gold Beach—Chowder Head Cook-off

May

Astoria—Clatsop County Timber Carnival
Newport—Loyalty Days Festival—Early
Florence—Rhododendron Festival—Middle
Astoria—Ship Model Competition—Middle
Brookings—Azalea Festival—Late
Depoe Bay—Fleet of Flowers—Late

June

Waldport—Beachcomber Days—Late
Astoria—Scandinavian Midsummer Festival—Late
Seaside—Sandcastle Contest—Late

July

Bandon—Old-Fashioned Fourth
Port Orford—Jetty Jubilee Celebration
Seaside—Independence Day Fireworks
Seaside—Miss Oregon Pageant—Middle
Yachats—Silver Smelt Fry—Middle
Newport—Lincoln County Fair—Late

August

Gold Beach—County Fair
Coos Bay—Haydn Festival—Early
Astoria—Clatsop County Fair—Early
Seaside—Beach Run—Middle
Coos Bay—Coos County Fair—Middle
Astoria—Regatta—Late

September

Depoe Bay—Indian-Style Salmon Bake—Middle
Coos Bay—Fun Festival—Middle
Bandon—Cranberry Festival—Middle

October

Yachats—Kite Festival—Middle

November

Seaside—Christmas Gift Fair—Late

December

Coos Bay—Orchid Auction—Early
Reedsport—Winter Storm Festival
Port Orford—Community Christmas Bazaar
Port Orford—Humbug Mountain Crafts Bazaar

Index